BLAZE A FIRE

SIGNIFICANT CONTRIBUTIONS OF CARIBBEAN WOMEN

Sister Vision

Black Women and Women of Colour Press

ISBN 0-920813-91-7

This book was produced by the collective effort of
SISTER VISION, Black Women and Women of Colour Press, Canada
in cooperation with
WOMEN AND DEVELOPMENT UNIT (WAND)
Extramural Department, University of the West Indies, Barbados
funded by INTER-AMERICAN and FORD FOUNDATIONS.

COVER ART AND DESIGN: Stephanie Martin
TYPESETTING: Ground Level Graphics
PRINTED AND BOUND IN CANADA

Haniff, Nesha Z. 1948-
  Blaze a fire

Includes bibliographical references.
ISBN 0-920813-91-7

1. Women — Caribbean Area — Biography. 2. Women —
Caribbean Area — Social conditions. 3. Caribbean
Area — Biography. I. Title.

HQ1501.H36 1988   305.4'09729   C88-095311-X

Published by
SISTER VISION
Black Women and Women of Colour Press
P.O. Box 217, Station E
Toronto, Ontario
Canada M6H 4E2

FOR PEGGY

Neck an neck an foot an foot wid man
She buckle hole her own;
While man a call her 'so-so rib'
Oman a tun backbone!

Louise Bennett

Table of Contents

WOMEN IN AGRICULTURE 17
Marie Grace Augustin 19
Ellen Jane Lindsey... 27
Flora Pascal 33
Saheedan Ramroop 39
Anjani Singh 45

WOMEN IN THE ARTS 53
Louise Bennett.. 55
McArtha Lewis 63
Edna Manley 69
Beryl McBurnie.. 77

WOMEN IN BUSINESS 85
Mable Tenn 87
Miss Tiny... 93
Olive Valmont 99

WOMEN IN THE CHURCH 105
Judith G. Weekes 107

WOMEN IN HEALTH 113
Sarah Baptiste... 115
Ruth Nita Barrow 121
Gweneth O'Reilly... 129

WOMEN IN ORGANIZATIONS 135
Nisa Ally 137
Millicent Iton 145
Ann Liburd 151

WOMEN IN POLITICS 157
Phyllis Shand Allfrey.. 159
Margaret Mary Dyer-Howe 165
Eugenia Charles... 171
Shirley Field-Ridley 177

WOMEN IN PUBLIC SERVICE 183
Desiree Bernard.. 185
Elaine Middleton 191
Louise Rowley... 197
Bernice Edna Yorke... 205
Isabel Sealy.. 211

GLOSSARY 217

Acknowledgements

I have had the good fortune to meet many of the great women of this region. These women have enriched and changed my life. This book is first for them. If a young person reads any of these profiles and is moved to emulate any of the women, or is able to see the great contributions of Caribbean women, then I will have accomplished what I set out to do. We of the Caribbean have come from a tradition of fine women — women of integrity, intelligence and spirit.

I take full reponsibility for the content of this book and therefore its drawbacks. The credit of this work is to be shared by many. My parents, Julie and Moudeen Haniff who raised me to respect myself and others. My sisters, Jean, Zela and Saudia are part of me. My nieces Sherifa and Annzalie and my nephews Raymon and Altaff are among the young people whose lives I hope will be touched by these women when they read about them.

Peggy Antrobus listened when I had the idea for this book. For this, and for many other reasons, including her unwavering struggle for women, I have dedicated this book to her.

Fitzroy Bryant insisted that I return to the Caribbean from North America. I shall always be grateful and love him for this.

Walter Allen, my best friend and my ally has always believed in my scholarship and supported me unequivocally. I can never repay him for his acts of friendship and faith in me.

Roderick Rainford has been unstinting in his support of this book. I am fortunate to know him.

These are the special people in my life who love me and who I love. For them saying thank you is contrived and artificial. I say it nonetheless.

The following are names of former and present staff members of the Women and Development Unit in Barbados where this project was based, and only some of the names of my very good friends and acquiantances who contributed to this book.

Sheila Leslie, Margaret Sardinah, Leslie Barrow-Whatley, Sandra Edwards, Pat Ellis, Ann Schwartz, Brenda Thomas, Joyce Harris, Norma Shorey-Bryan, Gloria O'Selmo, Veronica Duke, Sheila Thorpe, Debbie Moseley, Neville James, Earl John, Kenrick Seepersad, Angela Andrews, Florence Francis, Linda Bowen, Bob and Lee Hefner, Marjorie and Chubby Jackson, Bal and Ruby Ramdial, Aunty Rose, Ingrid and Dobrene O'Marde,

Stephanie Martin, Makeda Silvera, Sheila Stuart, Jeanette Bell, Carol Barrow, Mona Harvey, Diana Inniss, Mona Barrow, Doreen Brathwaite, Leo Hewitt, Vanda Radzik, Pat Rodney, Wanda Reid, Andaie.

Kathleen Drayton and Nan Peacocke constantly reassured me by sharing the struggle and the vision of *Blaze a Fire*.

This work was made possible by funding from the Inter-American and Ford Foundations.

To all those mentioned here and others too many to mention, I say these words of Jean Baptiste Massieu, the French ecclesiatic:

"La reconnaisance est la memoire de couer
Gratitude is the memory of the heart."

My heart remembers

NESHA Z. HANIFF
Ann Arbor
December 11, 1986

Preface

These remarkable stories record the active participation of Caribbean women in the economic, social, cultural and political development of our region. In so doing they refute the notion that men are the bread-winners and women the housewives, doing whatever they do under the leadership and direction of men. These stories then challenge the commonly held view of the sexual division of labour. They provide a picture of the social conditions of women's lives under capitalism in these former British colonies and this background gives insight into how gender attitudes are shaped by tradition and education.

The women, of different races and classes, who walk through these pages, illustrate the strategies they used for success in societies where, by and large, they were relegated to secondary status. Their lives and achievements are further evidence to dispel what Reddock (1984) calls two pervasive myths. The first of these is that "women have always been housewives secluded within the household" until brought out by the modernization process of the capitalist system. The second myth is "the view that the definition of women into the family has precluded their participation in social and political movements and struggle and made them a politically conservative and reactionary force." The lives of all these women are examples of struggle which has advanced our societies.

These stories are also a window to the moral value system of women and how it differs from male morality. Research in the United States has identified the different ways men and women respond to similar moral problems. They argue the existence of a male morality of individual rights and non-interference contrasted to a female morality of responsibility for universal rights and interdependence within the human community. All these women, visible and invisible, share a moral value system which recognizes the importance of inter-dependence. In upholding their particular moral view of social responsibility the women display courage, intelligence, strength and perseverance.

The "invisible" women are of particular significance in this book. What their stories show is the enormous contribution made to development by people who are considered unimportant, or, of low social status. Their presence in these pages compels a new look at history and at the use of the historical method.

I was moved and inspired by these stories of the achievements of "visible" and "invisible" Caribbean women. Their lives are important models for us to study in our attempts to discover what enables women to succeed.

I hope this book will find its way into the hands of the general public, but, more importantly into Caribbean schools, because there is no other text on this subject. At one level it provides a wealth of information about agriculture, commerce, the arts, politics, social sciences and the public service. At another level it provides material for exploration of social phenomena and moral issues.

This unique and imaginative book is an important contribution to our understanding both of ourselves as Caribbean women and of our role in development.

KATHLEEN DRAYTON

Faculty of Education
University of the West Indies
February 2, 1987

Introduction

The primary objective of this book is to instill in the reader a value of women and a value of Caribbean women. It is not that women are not valued, they are — as mothers, wives, helpers, and nurturers. And yet, women as intellectuals, business executives, labourers, organizational heads and farmers must be appreciated as well. Why are women not valued for these skills in the region's current school curricula? Perhaps it is because books are still largely written as though women exist on the periphery. In *The Making of the West Indies,* the principal history text for the last twenty-five years, the word woman appears only nine times. Surely women played a much more important part in "The Making of the West Indies"! Until women are fully integrated into the story of our history, our sociology, and our culture, publications like *Blaze a Fire* will continue to be necessary.

Twenty-eight women are profiled in this book: they are symbols of the achievement of all Caribbean women. They come from the twelve English-speaking countries of Antigua and Barbuda, Barbados, Belize, Dominica, Grenada, Guyana, Jamaica, Montserrat, St. Lucia, St. Vincent and the Grenadines, St. Kitts/Nevis and Trinidad and Tobago. As women, we too have shaped this region, and it is time for this to be documented and systematically included in the books and institutions which shape the minds of the people of this region. Some of the women here are known internationally and throughout the Caribbean and have been recognised for their great contributions. Most of the women, however, are known only locally and would only be recognised within their milieux, if at all.

At the heart of the many concerns raised by this book, is the essential issue of method. How can we include women in the events of history when their traditional work and roles are not viewed as central to the development of society? The problem for the recorders of history and for the describers of our society is how to fit the roles of women into this view of history. Should women be included separately or as part of the main body of documentation? It should be the latter, but to do this, the recorder must first recognise the importance of women, even though they may not be at what is now "the centre of the action." First the "centre" must be re-defined, so that both men and women can be seen as contributors to society. It is hoped that *Blaze a Fire* with other books, like *Lionheart Gal: Life Stories of Jamaican Women*, will influence the writings of not only the present recorders of our society but, more importantly, of the recorders to come.

We can see from these twenty-eight profiles that what women do is interesting and relevant to subjects like English Language, Literature, History, Business Studies, Agriculture, Tourism, Geography, Economics and Sciences. *Blaze a Fire* documents unequivocally that women contribute now and have historically contributed in all spheres of work in the Caribbean. They have been nurses and cane cutters, prime ministers and rice planters, intellectuals and religious leaders. Clearly the work in this region is done not only by office workers or teachers, or by doctors and lawyers, but by the banana farmers, and the planters of rice and cane as well. And this is in addition to the domestic and child care labour women have traditionally performed.

It is one of the objectives of this book to sensitize its readers to the issue of race in the Caribbean. Caribbean people are of European, African, Asian and Carib descent. Each person contributes, and the person is measured in this book by their commitment to their country, by their awareness of the problems women face and by their outstanding efforts at making a better life for themselves, their families and their communities. Caribs in this region are almost extinct. With them lies the remnants of a life that existed in the Caribbean before slavery and indentured labour. Women of Indian descent are vital to the survival of Guyana, Trinidad and the region generally. The fact that they have been overlooked and have been rendered invisible does not mean that they have made no significant contibutions.

We gain insight into the culture of this region from these women's lives. It is rich and is expressed in ways indigenous only to us, despite its various roots. The practice of susu is a Caribbean-wide practice: it is called "throwing partners" in Jamaica, "meetin' turn" in Barbados and "throwing box" in Guyana. The Indians in Trinidad and Guyana are Muslims and

Hindus; Eid and Phagwah are national holidays in these countries. Not only are there Christians, Muslims and Hindus in this region, but there are also Bahais and Buddhists. Caribbean readers can see and hear the similarities and differences between their countries in each profile. The voices here are the voices of each country as well as the voice of the region.

SELECTION OF THE WOMEN

Blaze A Fire does not claim to be the definitive work of Caribbean women's contributions. It is merely a start, there is much more to be done. The women in this book can be divided into two categories: "visible" women, who have a public presence and acknowledged status; and "invisible" women, whose contributions to society are made privately and who receive little public recognition for their work. Within these very large categories, women were selected for both their traditional and non-traditional work.

The selection of the "visible" women was easy. Since the project was based in the Women and Development Unit of the University of the West Indies (WAND), their field staff was consulted in compiling the list of "visible" Caribbean women. Each person named was discussed in terms of her contribution and her visibility. The list of "invisible" women was constructed through a series of informal contacts in community organizations. Through its regional operations over the years, WAND had developed contacts and relationships with community, governmental and church organizations in almost all the islands. A letter was sent to two community contacts in each island explaining the project and the kind of women that would be needed, indicating that the "invisible" woman's contribution had to be seen as important to her local community as that of a "visible" woman's to larger institutions.

The response to these requests was quite positive. Usually a committee to select the women was set up in each island, and would generate a list no longer than five women. The final selections were made by me. I asked various people at random in the countries of the "visible" women about their knowledge of these women. For the "invisible" women, this random check was made in their communities. Because of the wide range of the women's work to be featured, only one woman in each category of work was selected. In other words, if a nurse was chosen in St. Vincent another nurse would not be chosen in Dominica.

The book was divided into eight sections: Women in the Arts; Business; Agriculture; the Public Service; the Church; Organizations; Health; Politics. These are, of course, not the only areas in which women have made contributions. Women in sports have been very active, particularly in Netball, for example.

At one point, taking out the section "Women in Politics" was seriously considered. However, I have decided to include this section and take the risks involved. Women have, after all, begun to seize power, have begun to influence in a formal, institutional way the direction of the countries in this region. Jackie Creft, of Grenada, died because of her political affiliation. Political women are of consequence in this region and their presence cannot be denied.

These Caribbean women in *Blaze A Fire* are women to esteem. Touching their lives was a great experience. I was always overwhelmed by their hospitality, their nurturing, their strength and dominance. And always they were grateful and surprised by the attention paid to them by this project.

Flora Pascal walked for over an hour to meet me at the airport when I was leaving and gave me a bouquet of Antheriums that she herself had grown. Marie Grace Augustin, the planter, was ailing when we met, yet the day I spent with her, she seemed suddenly energized. For three years Beryl McBurnie refused to be interviewed because of the tape recorder. Finally, I called her up and said, "Beryl, I am here in Trinidad specifically to see you and I will wait at your door and not leave until you do!" She did see me and she was wonderful. She even got up, full of drama, and danced. I believe the most powerful woman I met was Saheedan Ramroop (Didi), the cane cutter. Perhaps I was impressed by her because she had none of the trappings of power — no official status, no education — yet no fear, none at all.

I recall that Flora Pascal was presented to me by the community group in Dominica as a housewife. One of the most devalued areas of women's work is domestic labour, so I wanted to include

Flora Pascal. She could not understand why I was putting her in a book; she was "just a housewife." I asked Flora what she did. She said:

— plant four acres of bananas
— sing in the choir
— decorate the church
— look after six children
— take care of the house
— sell home-made baked goods outside her home
— grow Antheriums for sale
— get up at three in the morning to walk one and a half hours to her farm and back
— additional chores like washing, ironing, etc.

And she was *just* a housewife. Silence about such women's lives makes them, and their work, invisible. The women presented here as outstanding may just be ordinary by Caribbean standards. But then I am a Caribbean chauvinist to think that outstanding is ordinary in this region.

Women in Agriculture

Women's first image is that of mother, housewife or nurse, not farmer or agriculturist. For many women in this region, farming is their profession of choice. The statistics range from country to country; for example in Montserrat, about 45% of the women farm. Farming then is as much a female occupation as it is a male occupation, and until this becomes acknowledged, women's farm work will continue to be seen as secondary to their real work as mothers and housewives.

Women farm, cut cane, plant rice and run plantations. These are all activities that the women profiled here inherited from their families. Ellen Jane Lindsey came from a family of farmers and she chose to farm because she genuinely loved it. Didi's mother was a cane cutter and Anjani Singh planted rice because it was her family's main economic activity. The same was true for Flora Pascal, the banana farmer. Marie Grace Augustin was a planter because she was the only one in her family who wanted to stay in St. Lucia and carry on the estate.

One gets a sense of the work of farming by looking at these women's lives. In them is a wealth of information and technology on planting their particular crop. The life of Ellen Jane Lindsey can serve as an excellent lesson in ecology and the development of technology appropriate for the environment. Didi's life in sugar is a lesson in the history of sugar in Trinidad and in the Caribbean. Marie Grace Augustin is a woman of historic importance to St. Lucia. Her life provides an excellent lesson in the history of the banana and coconut crops in St. Lucia. Through Flora Pascal we can look at the role of women in growing bananas.

These women were not only farmers, they were outstanding individuals. Didi was an advocate for workers and particularly for women. She was relentless in cases of sexual harassment. "Any woman in the field who come and tell me that about a foreman, I would make sure he never work there again." Didi delivered one of her children in the cane fields and went back to work the next day. Such stories illustrate the particular conditions of women workers. She struggled for maternity benefits and for the rights of all workers; her life tells the story of the role of women in unions in the region. One can see from these women's lives that hard manual labour is done by women. Cane cutting is seen as a male profession yet there have been women cane cutters in almost every sugar producing country in the Caribbean. Banana farming is done by women and they too, do their share in the harvesting of the bananas which involves heavy lifting. Ellen Jane Lindsey terraced her own farm on the mountainside. The lives of these women in agriculture, in Guyana, Trinidad and Tobago, Dominica, Montserrat and St. Lucia clearly show that women have farmed historically, have done the same heavy, back-breaking work as men, and have affected very profoundly the communities in which they lived.

Marie Grace Augustin

June 2, 1897
Planter
St. Lucia

Marie Grace Augustin was born in St. Lucia the seventh of eleven children. Until 1794, when it was captured by the British, St. Lucia was a French colony. The island is mountainous and like Montserrat, the mountains are densely forested. It was in this rural, romantic scenery that Grace Augustin was born on the 2nd day of June, 1897, on the estate of Daubayan. Her childhood in the early 1900s on the estate was carefree and happy. She was a tomboy and loved to swim and ride the cows bareback. She was an excellent horsewoman, and had at one time envisioned becoming a jockey. Her father was a planter and at that time the money-making crop was cocoa. Grace was an eager little girl. She always wanted to be in everything. Her brothers and sisters would tease her about being "too fast."

> I was the type to do whatever needs to be done. So much so that as a kid if my father and mother called to hand something to them or fetch something I would be the one to rush forward, you know. I want to do. I want to be the first to do this thing no matter what it was. Sometimes the bigger ones would say, not you, it is I, and get me out of the way. Eagerness to do, that was one of my qualities, of course I got into trouble too because of it. They used to speak of me as being 'too fast'. Oh that was a common thing for them to use on me. 'Oh you too fast.'

Her parents sent her to high school in Antigua, after which she returned to St. Lucia and decided to take up nursing. Her family had a home in Castries, the capital of St. Lucia, where she lived until 1930. She trained in Victoria Hospital for three years and became a nurse-midwife. While she was training there, her brother embarked on a career as a brilliant and successful lawyer. This attracted her and she apprenticed herself to a local lawyer so that she could prepare for her law exams.

> I did my three years training. When I was supposed to prepare for my examination I applied to the registrar who was responsible for this. To my surprise, he turned me down, because I was a woman.

This was around 1923, when the idea of a woman lawyer was indeed highly unusual. Grace Augustin had wanted to be a jockey, had wanted to be a lawyer and aspired also to be a cricketer. She did join the St. Lucia cricket club and was the only woman to do so.

> I joined the cricket club. I paid my dues and I would practice with the men. One day I went out to play and this big tall man, he was determined that this woman had no business on this field. He would bowl to me so fast, instead of sending the ball to the wicket he would send it to hit me. He thought I couldn't use a bat, but I was a very fine cricketer. I stayed because I joined that club and I had every right to be there.

Her life, at a very early age, had a non-traditional turn. All her brothers and sisters were getting married except her. She was interested in nursing and in the affairs of the estate. In the early 1930s the plantation was in financial trouble and the family had to sell their home in Castries. Grace took her mother and father back to the estate and began to run it herself. She was extremely interested in planting and embarked on a series of profitable crops that made her a successful and outstanding planter. Her brother had run the adjoining estate called Patience and when he died she ran both of them.

Times were rough and rustic. To get to Castries she had to ride eighteen to twenty miles on horseback. To supply everyone on the estate with provisions, she opened a grocery shop. To cater to the many guests that came through the area, she opened a guest-house. To meet the medical needs of the people on Daubayan, she opened a clinic, and to meet the need for furniture after the great fire in Castries in 1948 she trained workers on the estate to become cabinet makers. All these things made her essential and invaluable to her community. She was extremely popular because she would tend to the children's sores and deliver babies whenever she was called. Marie Grace Augustin was not only the rare female planter in the region but was a pioneer woman of St. Lucia.

Her pioneering activities were not only in the caring for the sick but in experimenting with new crops. She was one of the first to grow coconut on a large scale and tap into the copra industry. After copra, she started to plant bananas when a reliable system of shipping them was devised. At one point the banana trees were hit by a crippling disease and all the crops on the island were infected. It was Grace Augustin who took a sailboat to Guadeloupe to get new plants and start all over again.

> I had become very very interested in planting and I loved it too.

The years of planting and experimenting with the various crops made her an expert. She was known to all the officials in government and had become so essential to those who needed guidance in the agricultural sector that she was nominated a member of the St. Lucia legislature in 1954. In recognition of her outstanding work, she was awarded the Order of the British Empire. These awards were given annually by the British government to those deemed worthy whether they were in the colonies or in England. Most of the countries which have gained independence from England have now devised a system of national awards, as the British awards are no longer appropriate.

She served as a member of the legislature for thirteen years and became the head of many associations. She was Director of the Coconut Growers Association, Director of the Banana Association, Director of the Sugar Manufacturers Association, Director of Copra Manufacturing Limited and the first President of the St. Lucia Women's Association. These associations are only those she has headed. She has been a member of innumerable others, and has written articles, given lectures, and been the recipient of many awards and honours.

Grace Augustin has never married and has no children of her own. She has one "adopted" daughter and has been responsible for financing the education of many. A large part of her nursing career was devoted to the care and welfare of children. It was this inclination to nurture and care which made her take the faltering Daubayan estate and put it on its feet, and it was this characteristic which made her remain with her parents, caring for them until they died. One of her most painful experiences was seeing her mother die. She was very attached to her mother and remembers her as

a darling. She was not very demonstrative, but she loved us very much.

Ms. Augustin feels that her most significant contribution to St. Lucia has been in farming.

My opinions in the agricultural field had a great deal of weight, so perhaps that was where I was most useful. It seems to me after many years in the agricultural field my opinion was respected, at committee meetings and things of that kind. When I was leaving, in every case I was highly complimented for the contribution I had made. My first attempt at contributing anything at all was in nursing. What had satisfied me most of all was that we did make a contribution to the hospital as far as the nursing field was concerned.

Grace Augustin is ninety years old now and health problems limit her activities. But she is a lovely woman who must have been quite beautiful in her day. Her conversation scintillates as she recalls the big, tall, strapping bowler who wanted her off the cricket field, or riding bareback on the cows or traveling to England or making impromptu speeches.

> I have done more as a woman than I know of anybody else. I seem to have made opportunities to be useful to the community. I have climbed the ladder pretty high. I wasn't thinking of myself when I was climbing. I was climbing because there was something to do and I did it. But I did not expect that I would be so highly thought of. In fact, I wasn't conceited, just hard working. I liked to work and was honest enough not to want more than I was entitled to. Mine was a successful life. Difficult at times, but on the whole I ended up very well.

She lives in Castries with her sister Flo. The estate has been sold and she and Flo support each other emotionally and morally. They remember the days when they waged battle against diseases at Victoria Hospital and at the estate. Marie Grace Augustin's life has not been at all traditional.

She was a planter, a guest-house keeper, a nurse, a midwife, a furniture-maker, grocery store keeper, cricketer, member of the legislature and director of many agricultural associations. These were only some of the things she did. When asked why she did all these things, she replied:

> I'll tell you why I did all these things. It is very simple. I did all these things because they needed to be done.

Confidential

Draft

Patience,

St. Lucia, B.W.I.

9th May '57.

Dear Mr Thorp:

I have to acknowledge and thank you for your letter containing the confidential question.

I wish I had the humility, the selflessness, the courage and whatever else it takes to reply simply and truthfully: "no thank you, Sir. I do not deserve this."

But it gives me a feeling of ~~immense~~ satisfaction to infer from the proposition that you think me worthy and recommended me. Further, it is an honour

to the women of Sr Lucia which
I have no right to deny them.
Lastly, were I permitted to ~~consult~~ refer this matter
to my family, I believe it would give
~~some~~ pleasure.

The answer, therefore, is that I ~~would~~
gratefully accept such an award.

~~Yours~~ Very sincerely yours,

Grace

Ellen Jane Lindsey

August 13, 1944
Farmer
Montserrat

Because Montserrat is so mountainous, many of the farmers farm on the mountainside which is often steep and rocky. Ellen Jane Lindsey farms on one of these difficult mountainsides. In 1980 she was judged Montserrat's farmer of the year. A natural farmer, she planted her first sweet potato at the age of four.

> I used to go with my grandmother and I notice everything she do. So one day I pick up a little piece of potato vine. So I said I goin to plant this little piece of vine, and she told me to

ahead, plant it, so I did. A few months after, she went to that
some vine and she got a big potato, that she had to put it on
my head and send it to the baker, and it was so big that it
share for everybody at home. It was a sweet potato. I feel
good and it give me an encouragement.

Ellen was born in St. Patrick, Montserrat, on the 18th of August
1944. She comes from a family of farmers. She received her first
lessons in farming from her grandmother.

> After I planted the potato I noticed that she would not plant
> on a small spot. So I told her that I going to work that spot,
> she said that I could work it but whatever I plant is not going
> to come out because it showl (shallow). I told her I still going
> to try it. Well I did try it. She gave me a few cotton seeds and
> I plant it and they come out good, and after a little while, just
> as she said, they died.

Planting the potato and cotton were Ellen Lindsey's first lessons.
Her family were small farmers and it was difficult for a family with
six children to survive on farming alone, sharing the family land.
Ellen was sent to live with a family in the same manner, and for
similar reasons, as Nurse Baptiste. Her responsibility in this family
was to oversee the younger children. When she came home from
school she would have to stay indoors when she wanted to go
outside to plant peas or tomatoes. It was a passion with her, the
planting. Every time the children's mother would leave, Ellen
would go outside and do some gardening. Sometimes she would
be caught and punished. But Ellen hated the confinement and
not being able to plant.

> Sometimes when she gone to town, I would call some of the
> children and say 'Come, let's fork up the place.' They come
> and we all work together, and when we finish we do some
> more. Well I studying now that when she came back I will get
> licks because I gone outside. But I still feel to do more work,
> so I take a hoe and hoe up de place. Then I get some corn,
> peas and plant it because when she come and she beat me I
> don't mind because the peas in the ground going to soon
> burst, so at least I'll have peas so it never used to trouble me.

She went as far as primary school and even there she excelled
in planting. There was a class which required that students learn
gardening and Ellen was able to get a plot of her own.

The boys used to plow the ground and the girls plant and weed. Well the boys didn't want to do any work, so teacher Mary took the bed and hand it over to the girls. Well I always lucky to get the worst, so they gave me the flattest bed and I take it. I saw my father had some little onions so I took up a few and I planted half of the bed. I went down to Mrs. Irish, I saw some dry red beans on the floor, so I told her please to give me and she say they weren't good but if I want them take them, and I take them and plant them at school. Every morning I water them, every afternoon I water them and everything start growing nice. Those red beans came nice and they start to run so I put some sticks for them to run on. One morning I go and see nothing. Somebody went and thief out everything, everything. Somebody go in and pull out all the onion and all the peas, Me never get a thing out of it.

This experience did not change her mind about farming.

I feel funny, but I still don't give up.

The home in which she lived required that she not only take care of the children but do housework, sell in the market and transport on her head large quantities of produce to the market as well. Meanwhile she continued to go to school.

Like if I come in with a bunch of plantain they give me 25 cents. And I still used to save every 25 cents under a glass and when it reach about $2.00 I bring it out and give my mother, was enough to buy me a dress then.

After she left school Ellen did several jobs while continuing her gardening. She worked as a seamstress' helper for a short while, and then worked for somebody else selling produce in the market. Her first wage was three dollars a week, but Ellen thought that this was too little so she negotiated a raise.

She said she will give me four dollars but I have to buy my lunch. Things were very cheap at that time because you could get a soft drink for 8 cents and a bread for 4 cents so seventy five cents could keep me for the week.

At eighteen, Ellen Lindsey got married and started a family of her own. By this time she had left her selling job, and she started to farm in earnest. The land in their family was shared out between her two brothers and a sister. Hers was a difficult one to farm because rocks and pebbles in the land had to be dug out. She was able to grow cucumber, cabbage, dasheen, peas and egg-plant. Meanwhile she started to raise sheep and goats and ac-quired a donkey. This was her means of transportation to the farm. It was two hours away and on an incline. She took on more plots; in all, she farmed two acres. She started to sell her pro-duce. The first time she sold the items she had grown she made forty-seven dollars and fifty cents. She knew that she was a good farmer. Somehow she was able to avoid the problems other farmers were having.

It was this awareness that made her enter her first agricultural exhibition. The first year she entered peas and won second prize in her category; the next time she entered dasheen, ginger and peanuts and won prizes for all. She entered her produce every time the exhibition was held and continued to win prizes. In 1980, her produce brought several firsts and she won the farmer of the year prize. In order to be eligible for this prize, the judges had to visit her plots. They were struck by the methods she used in irrigating her plots and protecting them. Because her land was difficult, it entailed the removal of rocks and terracing. This is a method farmers in mountainous or hilly countries use. When the land is on an incline, everything is washed away when it rains. In order to prevent this, a system of terracing is used. These are step-like constructions along the side of the hill. The flat steps are used for planting, and are held in place by rocks or other materials. The judges were impressed by Ellen Lindsey's terrac-ing particularly since she used the materials available to her. The rocks and bricks that she pulled out of the soil to make it arable were used to construct the terraces. All of this she did herself by hand with no heavy equipment. Producing such fine crops was quite a feat and the craft and skill in organizing such dif-ficult land were very impressive.

> I didn't know that I had won this, is not until the prize-giving
> ceremony that I come to know and it make me feel good,
> proud, to know that it was from me hands that this happen.

Ellen Jane Lindsey loves farming. It gives her a deep sense of satisfaction. It is how she expresses herself. Farming, like any other profession, requires skill and a great deal of knowledge.

Many women farm in the Caribbean, but are considered gardeners — people who plant on small plots for their own consumption. The difference between farming and gardening is seen in terms of size and intent. If planting is done full time on a large enough scale as the basic means of a livelihood, then this is thought of as farming. This view was held by agricultural programs, extensions and exhibitions. The plots that women farm are often their only means of making a living, and the plots are often small because, generally, women do not own or are not normally able to lease large areas of land for planting purposes. This does not mean that women are not farmers. Ellen Lindsey was able to overcome the size issue by using the land in her family and by leasing additional plots, not because she could afford them, but because she had a passion for farming. Fortunately, she was able to make it work.

Farming for Ellen Jane Lindsey is special, it is not just a job, or something that she has to do. It is something that brings her self-respect and pride. Farming is her way of being creative, of being productive, of being independent and being religious. For her, to farm is to meditate.

> I really like agriculture. Farming is a good thing because you could feed yourself and make yourself independent and people don't have to push you around. When I plant I feel close to God, because while I there I meditate with God, you in you garden by yourself, you just feel good, at one with God. Farming is good. It is just as good as going out to work or teaching children in a school.

Flora Pascal

1930
Banana Farmer
Dominica

It was August, 1979, the wind was howling and the rain was beating down on the tin roof of Flora Pascal's house. There was a knock on the door; it was Mr. Bryce, the next door neighbour, who had come over to say that the hurricane was serious. Flora Pascal thought that it would blow over, that the eye of the hurricane would be at sea. She soon realized how very unprepared they were for the hurricane. She was sure that their house was going to collapse. Already, galvanized sheets were being ripped off of the roofs of houses by the hurricane. They were sailing in the air at speeds that could decapitate a person if hit. Flora began to cook so that they could at least have enough to eat. Afterwards she took some food for neighbours whose roofs had blown off and who were scurrying for shelter. She then went to check on her animals, she thought most of them would die. She saw about four of them and untied a couple more. When she returned home her husband and sons were able to climb on top of the roof and nail it down. All these things were done in wind and rain that was blowing at over one hundred miles per hour. Her house battered by the wind and rain shook and trembled and shook some more. It did not fall even though it was on stilts. The hurricane was the worst in Dominica's history. Flora Pascal and her family survived it with their home intact and enough food to eat. They were among the lucky few.

Perhaps this survival was not undeserved because Flora Pascal left her house to help others. This is something that she has always done, hurricane or not.

Flora Pascal lives in the village of Marigot and was born in Dominica in 1930. She is a village leader. Many Dominicans make their living by growing bananas and other fruit and vegetables. Flora and her husband made their living by growing bananas. However, they have never had land of their own, they planted the land of a relative who then sold it to someone else. They were then left with no means of making a livelihood. The only thing they knew was planting. Her husband found a job on the estate as a labourer and she worked as a domestic, became a seamstress, baked tarts and other treats and sold them on a tray. In addition, she grew tomatoes, cabbage and other vegetables for their own consumption and for sale. She raised a few goats, chickens and sheep. They made ends meet but they were banana planters and planting bananas was how they survived. They decided to plant on government land. No sooner had they started to plant than the government officials came and asked them to leave. This did not make sense to Flora Pascal; they were unemployed, why couldn't they plant bananas?

They returned to the government land and continued to plant. This time they were able to reach an agreement with the officials. They were able to work out a system of owning the land.

Flora Pascal plants four acres of bananas. Her husband continues to work as a labourer and also works on the banana farm but it is she who carries the brunt of it. She plants the seeds, spreads the fertilizer and harvests the bananas. Harvesting is a very difficult and strenuous job because it requires cutting the bunch of bananas from the tree, lifting the bunch and carrying them to their assigned stacking point.

The banana farm is an hour and a half walk from where she lives, and she goes to the farm every day. This means that her day starts at four-thirty in the morning. By the time she arrives at the farm it is six in the morning. After her work is over, there is the hour and a half walk back. But Flora Pascal's day is not filled with a three-hour walk to and from work, or looking after the banana trees or tending the anthuriums she plants. On Saturdays she must decorate the church for Sunday service. Then she must attend choir practice because she sings in the church choir. She also teaches catechism once a week as well as helping organize Sunday service. Apart from her joining the church activities she is an active member of the Social League which involves visiting the sick and caring for those less fortunate. She attends all meetings be they church committee meetings or the Social League meetings.

> From the time I joined the Social League, the theme of it was
> to build up the community and your own self. From that time
> I would always attend meetings. I would go out visiting the
> sick. When I visit the sick I would clean, go for water, wash
> and so on. We do it in groups but by myself I still go and do
> different things, give the people whatever I have. In meetings I
> always try to be there, to help in any difficulties with anybody.
> I like to be of help.

Flora Pascal came from a poor family of eight children. Her mother could not take care of them all and Flora was raised by another family. She herself got married in 1954 and had five children. Her life has been a long hard struggle — typical of the life that many rural women lead in the Caribbean. She is a leader in her community because she feels compassion for those who are struggling and less fortunate and because she acts on that compassion. She involves herself in all the activities that help her village.

> I try to do my best. It had always been in me to help. I see
> the way I was struggling and I see others come and struggling
> so I say to myself by helping one another we can come
> together — togetherness, which we need a lot.

A caring, active person who takes responsibility soon builds
up a reputation as reliable. If there is a bazaar or church activity
or an illness, Flora Pascal is called. If there is a death or a wedding or a christening, Flora Pascal is there. Flora Pascal does
everything and is the pivot of most of the village activities.

> Well, God has given me so many talents. I could so do many
> different things. I try to help other people and help myself.

Yet such a person can be so relied upon that it creates com-
placency in others. Everyone knows that Flora Pascal will be at
the meeting, will visit the sick, will decorate the church, will clean
the church, will do whatever is necessary. As a result, others come
to feel that they could shirk their responsibilities.

> We plan our own service for Sundays, and I am one of them
> making the program. We are supposed to meet every
> Wednesday afternoon and several Wednesday afternoons I
> went and the people were not there as though they were
> playing some hide and seek. I would have to say that it is
> more young people. So I said well maybe the young people
> feel I am too old to be with them, but still they want me to
> help in other things. I decided that I would just quit
> everything and see what they would do.

She stopped going to meetings, did not decorate the church,
stopped her involvement in the Social League and did not go to
church. The whole village was in a state of shock. Flora Pascal
not being involved, not being their cornerstone? They could not
believe it.

> When I stayed home one or two days a child would come and
> say, why you didn't come to church? Another person would
> say but I didn't see you in church how many Sundays now? I
> said how you mean? I am not coming back to the church
> man, you are all too hypocrite, I am not coming back. People
> have to be fair, you have to be good in the community. The
> way you all getting on I am not coming back. When Sister
> Maria came back they told her that I wasn't at church, and
> she knows fully well once I am there everything will be

alright, decoration, cleaning and everything. Everyone start to inquire about me and when they ask me I said you all are too hypocrite and I do not want to be as you all. Can't be just going out, I have so many things to do, wastin' my time and you people are just sportin'. They still calling on me. Saying I must come, I must come back. They don't know what to do. They have to buy flowers to decorate the church because I grew flowers so I always brought mine. All this is giving them a headache.

Flora Pascal stayed out of these activities on purpose. She wanted the people to take responsibility for their community and not to take her own participation for granted.

I feel people should help each other. It should not be on one person alone. You must be an example in the community that they must see light in you as a leader. Some of us say we are leaders and really people don't see it through us, but right now I can say they are really seeing it in me. From I start to work they can see it. When I stayed away from the church I realized that the people really looked at me as a leader.

The village of Marigot survives on its farming and on its people; one cannot exist without the other. Flora Pascal is essential to both in her community. The church and the Social League depend on her. She plants four acres of bananas, raises goats and rabbits, and anthuriums, bakes, sews, cares for the elderly and the sick and carries on a household. She is a short, shy woman whose hands are strong and rough. She is kindly and speaks openly. She is the leader of her village and the light that everyone looks to.

Flora Pascal continues to work hard and struggle like everyone else. She has nothing to give but her time and herself and she in turn gets nothing but satisfaction and self-respect. These are simple things and in the small village of Marigot these simple things make Flora Pascal a special human being.

Saheedan Ramroop

February 14, 1922
Cane-Cutter
Trinidad and Tobago

I n Caribbean families of East Indian Origin, brothers and sisters called their eldest sister Didi. In her family and in her village of Eldorado in Trinidad this is what Saheedan Ramroop was called — Didi, the eldest sister. This name for an elder sister is now becoming a thing of the past. In the Sugar Workers Union she is known as Sister Saheedan.

Didi is a cane-cutter. She was born on February 14, 1922. She started to work in the cane fields when she was ten years old.

This means that she has presided over all the changes that have come to the sugar industry in Trinidad in the last fifty years. She recalls that at the beginning:

> Workers had no rights. You had no rights neither from management, neither from union. Overseers kick you, drivers kick you, you have nothing to say. We was slaves here on de estate. I see how they treat we. I witness that eh. I remember I was in de canefield weedin and this old man and this old lady was working in Orange Grove and when they workin de driver come and say that he want the edge on the drain white as a kerchief. De old lady say, 'but this is dirt, how dirt could be white.' He say 'don't back talk me' and he give that woman one kick, and she fall down and he kick she again. The next man say, 'but that is advantage, you take and kick that poor woman.' The driver turn around and chase that man. That man had to jump forty drain before that driver stop chasin. That man never work in that section again after that.

This treatment of workers politicized Didi and motivated much of her concern for her fellow workers and villagers. As late as the 1960s many people felt that the Sugar Workers Union was corrupt. Workers who were caught trying to organize or agitate were harassed and punished by the union. Didi nonetheless held meetings at her home. This fearlessness is the overwhelming characteristic in Didi's personality. She is described by the leader of the union as one of the most fearless organizers and mobilizers of people in the union. Both her activities as union organizer and cane-cutter are non-traditional for women. Didi is also unusual because she is a shop steward, a leadership position not commonly held by women.

The other side of Didi's non-traditionality is her job as cane-cutter. Although women do work in the sugar industry, it is primarily as weeders and water-carriers. Cane-cutting is done mostly by men. They say it is because it requires a physical strength that women do not have. There are examples that refute this. Saheedan Ramroop is one. But Didi is not the only one; there are small brigades of female cane-cutters in almost every Caribbean country where sugar is grown. Quite often these jobs are very well paid. A cane-cutter, for example, is one of the highest paid field workers in the sugar industry. Although it is men who cut cane as a general rule, it is important that the existence of female cane-cutters be known much more widely. This information should dispel the notion that women cannot cut cane or do jobs which require physical strength.

Didi is an interesting mixture of passionate commitment, the unorthodox, and the heroic. She was the major instigator of the famous 1973 Tello-Hunt strike in Trinidad. She was in the front lines of the march for higher wages for sugar workers in 1975. During that march she was hit and injured in the melee between police and workers. Didi cannot read or write but will confront management on any issue of injustice. There is a famous story about Didi during the 1975 strike that is bound to become a folk legend in union history in Trinidad.

The workers were beginning to feel the effects of the long strike, they were grumbling and wanted to go back to work. They were tired of the struggle and the sacrifices required of them. A meeting was called to reinforce the workers, to remind them of what they were fighting for. Didi was at this meeting. She was listening to the union leader trying to encourage the workers. She herself had seen so much. She had known the time when workers were treated as slaves, when they lived on twenty-five cents per day, when they lived in mud houses, existing on very little. They had come so far and struggled so hard and now they were buckling under pressure. She found this intolerable.

> Look like you put a blaze a fire in me and it blaze, it burnin me to know that we trying to get betterment and these man them breaking and they rebelling.

Didi was so outraged that she jumped up and grabbed the microphone from the speaker. She said:

> Women have belly and they would stand up, and all you man only study to go inside the rum shop. All you who want to go, go, cause all you dis is worms feedin on de union. We suffer so long here, and we must sacrifice, and if we have to eat dirt we must eat it, and if we have to eat brick we must eat it, before we go back to that condition we was in, and if we have to eat grass we will eat grass.

As she said this, she bent down and furiously pulled a clump of grass and ate it. The workers were stunned by this act. They were moved by Sister Saheedan and continued the strike until their demands were met. The Union Leader, at that time Mr. Basdeo Panday, recalled this moment and described it as the most dramatic and effective act in continuing the strike.

Didi has had ten children; her husband is a sugar worker as well. When they got married, they lived in a house made of mud. Today they have built a large home in its place with the help of a bank loan. Didi has other property which she has accumulated over the years as well. This could not have happened without both their incomes. In most instances in the Caribbean, it takes more than one income to purchase or build a house. Didi accumulated her property mostly on her initiative. A cooperative effort is required in most families to buy homes, furniture and appliances, and in many cases, it is the women who make these investments. They are able to do this by being innovative and thrifty. One of the ways is a cooperative female savings system called "susu." There are various names for this throughout the Caribbean, for example in Guyana it is called "throwin box." It was this system of accumulating capital that Didi used to make her modest purchases over the years.

Susu is an informal saving system among women. The number of women ranges from three to fifteen. The women would each contribute a specific sum of money on an arranged schedule. For example they would decide to each contribute twenty dollars per week with the pay off date every month or two months. If there are five women in a susu then in a week a sum of one hundred dollars will be collected. The idea is that each woman will get a turn at collecting a sum of money. In some places this sum of money is called a "hand." For example, the women decide that they would "draw a hand" every month. This would be done until each woman has had her turn. If there are five women and a "hand" is every month, then the susu will last five months. Each monthly hand will be four hundred dollars. Susu has one woman as its axis. She keeps the money until the "hand" is ready and makes sure that every one gets their turn. She must be reliable and trustworthy. Didi has always been the person for female co-workers and villagers who "they throw susu or box with." "Throwin susu" with Didi means not only that a specific sum of money is guaranteed but that they have a person who will guide them in their expenditures. If the women want to use their "susu money" to put a new roof on, add a room or fix the kitchen, Didi becomes their guide. She finds a reliable carpenter, assists them in the purchase of building material and so on. She, like nurse Baptiste, is essential to her village. The rituals of birth, death and marriage are incomplete without her presence.

This leadership is not one that was conferred on Didi. She earned it. She did so by responding to those in need, by keeping her word at all times, by always advocating for those weaker than herself and by simply being herself. She lets very little pass, and will confront you immediately. This is not always a pleasant experience. But it is this same forthrightness which makes her a leader who the people trust implicitly.

Like many other Caribbean women, Didi has spent her life in hard physical labour. She mothered ten children, became a union steward and a spokesperson for her fellow workers. Two of her children were born in the cane-field. Not only did she work in the field until delivery; she also returned to work the next day. This experience was not uncommon among women who worked as manual labourers. Every day away from work meant a loss in the pay that was crucial to maintaining their families. As part of the struggle for workers' rights, women in the sugar industry now have maternity benefits which would allow them to stay home up to three months after delivery. Didi was one of those who agitated for this. Today, throughout the Caribbean, maternity benefits are available only to some working women; it is something that still has to be struggled for.

Her commitment to elevating the conditions of other sugar workers is absolute. Because of her assertiveness and high activist profile, she has been offered the job of field foreman at least four times over the years. This job would take her out of the manual labour category and increase her salary. She rejected these offers unequivocally.

> I say I will never, never take it, they ask me why is de reason. I say no because you have to do what management say. You have to be pressurizing you own poor people and ah don't want to do that, I will never do that.

Some people might describe Didi as a feminist — and rightly

so. She feels that women are discriminated against in the sugar industry.

> Is woman have to do all the work. If is plant cotton, is woman, if to turn plant, is woman, if is to throw salt is woman. It ain't have a work to do is not woman, Dey ain't have woman in de factory. Man sit down and sew bag, woman could do that. No woman workin in de pen, woman could do that, all of we does mind animal. All de factory work they ain't have woman, da ain't right.

Her life can be seen in three major categories, as a worker, as a union organizer, and as an advocate for women. On reading about Didi, one would think that she is a tall, strong and massive woman. She is not. She is a Hindu woman who performs her puja every day, and who wears an orhni when she gets dressed up. Dressed in her orhni, one would think she is just a 'nice' Trinidad Indian lady. There is no conventional clue to the fearlessness she embodies, or the love, trust and esteem with which she is regarded.

> Ah don't like to see nobody advantage nobody. Anytime I see that I does jump in. If my child is doin something wrong I say is damn wrong. Wrong is wrong. Ah say is me alone goin in my box you know man. No husband, no children, nobody ain't goin with me. Is me and me alone, is only one Saheedan Ramroop in de whole Orange Grove estate you know man. Is me and me alone have that mind. So I don't want to go with nobody.

There is only one Saheedan Ramroop, not only on the Orange Grove Estate where she works, but in her village and in her union. She is an activist woman who cuts cane, who walks barefoot, and who can neither read nor write. She allowed none of these things to impede her. Had she had a formal education, her sense of justice, her passion and her commitment would have made her a national leader.

There are those who say that management is afraid of Didi because of her power. They say that if she were to walk in the cane-field and say "Put down you cutlass we goin on strike," that without question all cutlasses would fall with one resounding clink.

Anjani Singh

October 3, 1933
Rice-Planter
Guyana

A njani Singh was born on Blairmont Estate on October 3, 1933.
She is Guyanese. Guyana and Trinidad are the two Caribbean
countries with large populations of East Indian descent. In the
1930s and 1940s when Anjani Singh was growing up, the status
of Indian women was determined primarily by their age and their
children. The women with power were usually grandmothers and
mothers-in-law. In addition to a societal esteem of the elderly,
these women administered large households, making decisions

that affected the lives of their children and their spouses. In most cases, the grandmother and the mother-in-law was the same person. A young woman who was newly married had the lowest status in this structure. She had no children and had left her parents' home to become part of her husband's family, where her life was directed by her mother-in-law and her husband. She evolved out of this relationship as she bore sons and herself became a mother-in-law and grandmother. Women then gained importance in direct relation to their sons. Daughters did not provide an avenue to status and power except through their ability to have sons.

Women as well as men were raised in a closely structured kinship society and their lives were dictated by the rules that regulated it. These rules limited roles for women who had to wait until their sons grew up to gain power and status or who by their own courage and creativity bent the rules so that their own needs could be accommodated. Anjani Singh's life is an example of such courage and creativity. It should be kept in mind that she was born in 1933 in a rural area and that her life spans the many changes that have come to the Indo-Guyanese community, particularly to the status of women.

Anjani's mother became ill when she was thirteen. Since she was the eldest daughter, she had to leave school and assume her mother's household responsibilities. This was in 1946 when a girl's education was not of great importance. At that time it was quite often the fate of many girls, particularly the eldest daughter, to take over all domestic duties. After a year Anjani's mother recovered from her illness. Anjani continued to stay at home but in the afternoons took lessons from the local seamstress. For a young woman, learning to sew was at the time an essential skill, a housewife who could sew saved money by making her own and her children's clothing. Buying ready-made clothes was not the norm. One had to have a seamstress or tailor make the clothes.

Anjani was now fifteen and the next step was marriage. It was common for girls to be married immediately after reaching puberty, but social changes had already begun to have an effect. In 1949, she got married at the ripe old age of sixteen. Her marriage to a cane-cutter in the same village was arranged by her parents. Arranged marriages are custom in many areas of the world including India and Africa. To many, an arranged marriage might seem cold and forbidding. In dominant western culture it is felt that marriage should come from falling in love, the wedding being a romantic affair. This is a concept of love and marriage that is foreign in many cultures. Marriage is viewed as a contractual matter that requires serious thinking and arrangement. The income level, reputation, home, assets and family involved are always carefully considered in arranging the marriage of a young man or a young woman.

There are many advantages to arranged marriages. Since the family takes responsibility in arranging the wedding, they also take responsibility in assisting the couple financially and emotionally. A person in an arranged marriage bases her expectations of that marriage on duty rather than love. The two enter into matrimony with expectations of having children, running a home, being responsible to parents as they grow older and weaker, growing old together and seeing their own children settled. Of course, an arranged marriage does not preclude love. Studies of successful love marriages have shown that these marriages are very similar in character to successful arranged marriages. Both parties have a realistic concept of work, home, place and family and both exist in a supportive kinship environment.

It was with such an orientation that Anjani Singh got married. She lived with her husband at his parents' home immediately after marriage. There were twelve other people living in this house; his brothers and their wives, his parents and their other unmarried children. Before her marriage the only work that Anjani did was housework. Though she was sixteen and married she was still a child. The month after her marriage, her mother-in-law took her to the rice field. The family that she married into was a rice-farming family even though her husband worked in the sugar cane industry. The first day that she went to the rice field she played with the mud and water and made mud toys. This marked her first exposure to rice-farming. No one could guess, looking at this child play, that she was to become a woman who would work eight acres of rice, build her own home and own over one hundred head of cattle.

Her mother-in-law fretted that she went to the rice-fields and played. This embarrassed Anjani and so she returned the next day and had her sister-in-law teach her the mechanics of rice-farming. She learned to throw seeds, protect the seeds from the birds and finally to plant. She learned quickly and soon became the best worker in the whole family. She was invaluable to them because she worked hard and rapidly. They were able now to plant more fields and increase the family income. Although her husband worked in the cane-fields he would come and help her whenever he could.

The hardest time of the year was the harvest season. Rice planting was done in a cooperative system. Each field would be planted by a group who individually owned or rented one or two fields. They helped plant each other's fields in order to minimize labour expense. However, at harvest time, additional workers would be needed to bag the rice and send it off to the factory to be milled. At this time Anjani would have to both supervise and work with about six men. There were some things that irked Anjani as she worked and contributed to the family. She received one-third of whatever was made even though she was responsible for the bulk of the work. She wanted to branch out on her own to work her own fields, and to live in her own home. One day as she and her husband were working, a family friend called her husband to have a private conversation. He said:

> Man look, I like de way you wife and you work. You not contentious people. I going to give you a chance and if you want you could take it.
>
> What you talkin about?
>
> I have a place I want to sell.
>
> Why you want sell it?
>
> Me not able to maintain the whole place, and I need some money to send me big boy to England.
>
> Well you come home by me we goin to discuss it.
>
> I goin discuss it too.

When he returned, Anjani said:

> What he want?
>
> He say we is quiet people and he want sell we a place, if we want to take de chance.
>
> Well if you get money you could buy it. Is a good chance.

>Girl where me going get money? Me going sell me shirt and pants?
>
>Me don't have money, but me going take de chance. Me going to sell me frock.
>
>Man you jokin and dis man serious.
>
>Me ain't jokin. I serious.
>
>Where you going get money?
>
>I going get money.

That afternoon after they had finished working, Anjani took a bath, changed her clothes and took a bus to her parents' home. They were surprised to see her. When her Aunt saw her she said:

>Gal, what happen, wha you come fa?

Anjani then told her aunt what had transpired that day and her aunt encouraged her to discuss it with her parents. After she told her mother and father, they immediately sent for her eldest uncle who was the family mentor. He said:

>She want it and if all you have it you must help her. She is trying to get on her own. Is nice to get on your own.

Her father then turned to her and said:

>Well how much so?

Anjani said:

>Bout five hundred so.
>
>Gal where me go get five hundred dollars from?

Her mother at this point spoke up and said to her husband:

>Well how much you get?

Her father then opened an old ovaltine can where he kept his money. He had three hundred dollars in the can. He turned to his wife and said:

>You go and see how much you get now.

Her mother said:

>Well, with you father three hundred, I will put two hundred.

When Anjani returned home, she told her husband about the money. They decided to tell his parents at once that they were going to buy their own place and eventually move out. Her mother-in-law was not pleased by the news and said that she had no money to give to them. Anjani's husband said:

Well, if you don't have is alright. We will still buy it.

His mother was surprised at this and asked:

Where you get money from?

Me na get is me wife get.

It was clear that his mother was surprised and ruffled by this news. His father intervened and said to his wife:

They want to get their own, let them try, is a good then to get on their own.

His son turned to him and said:

Pa you goin help me?

Boy where me go get money from ... Alright when de time meet me going see if me could sell a cow and give you de money.

Anjani Singh wanted her own home; this was her chance and she seized it. She was a young woman who had little control over her life and her earnings. Her own self-confidence and vision and her ability to utilize her familial network helped her find the courage and creativity to become independent.

The land they bought was full of bushes and needed to be bulldozed before they could build. The only way to do this was to ask an Englishman who was in charge of a building project in that area. She went to ask the man the cost of bulldozing her land. He was so impressed by her boldness in coming to him herself that he did not charge her. The land was bulldozed the day after it was bought. Anjani knew that the workmen who cleared the land did it after their work hours were over. She wanted to let them know that she appreciated what they were doing. She went home, made dal puri, channa and chicken curry and bought three bottles of rum so that the workmen could at least have a meal and a drink. Her husband was astounded when he came from the cane field and saw their property. He said: "Well girl you is somethin eh."

They did not move right away. She continued to live with her mother-in-law and began accumulating building materials for the house. At that time she became pregnant and had her first child. Meanwhile she continued to plant and harvest rice. In order to build the house they took a loan from the sugar estate where her husband worked. As they paid this loan Anjani decided that it was time for her to have her own rice-field. This would give her control over her livelihood. Previously she had rented a rice-field. Having accumulated a small down payment, she decided that it was time to use the rent money to own the land rather than rent it.

They moved into their new home with their own rice-field. They had a loan and a rice-field to pay for but no furniture. These expenditures made Anjani's income critical. She wanted to furnish her house and paint it. Instead she bought two cows. No one could understand that, but Anjani had in mind to raise and sell the cows and their milk. Her mother-in-law gave her a cow which in turn gave birth to a heifer. The cows, their milk, and the rice along with her husband's income from sugar would combine to generate enough income to pay the debts and afford whatever else was needed.

Through her initiative and courage, Anjani Singh sold and raised over one hundred head of cattle. She planted more than eight acres of rice and delivered milk to numerous people in the area. She had six children while she was in the process of carving out this life for herself. Her day started at 3:30 A.M. She got up, woke her husband, made his breakfast, soaked the wash for the day, took her bath and then delivered milk. When she returned she tidied the house, made the children's breakfast and then left for the rice-field at 7:00 o'clock.

Her ambition was to become independent and to do this she worked hard.

> You must work hard. When you work hard and you get you own money, you will be more independent, and when you want to do something, you have you own money. You don't have to go ask nobody.

Anjani Singh is not a rich woman. Her vision was to become independent, have her own house, and be able to take care of herself and her family adequately. She was able to achieve all of this primarily through her own initiative.

She is a diminutive woman with marvelous eyes. She raised her head and looked at the world around her and saw a life of toil and hard work ahead. When the time came to choose, to take a chance, she had nothing but her strength, her courage and the frock she was wearing and she chose:

> Me don't have money, but me goin take de chance. Me goin sell me frock.

Women in the Arts

The women profiled in this section are all pioneers of their art form. Edna Manley is the mother of the Jamaican Art Movement. She sculpted and worked in art in Jamaica when it was lonely and difficult. Beryl McBurnie is the mother of Trinidad and Caribbean Dance and it was the house where she was born that became the Little Carib Theatre. Louise Bennett pioneered the art form of the Jamaican language and Calypso Rose was the first woman to win all the calypso titles in Trinidad and Tobago. Phyllis Shand Allfrey is known in literary circles for her book, *The Orchid House*, but she is in this book as a woman in politics.

There are, outside of Phyllis Shand Allfrey, no other writers in this book. The Caribbean, of course, is known for its writers. Among some internationally known women writers are Paule Marshall, Jamaica Kincaid and Jean Rhys. There are, of course, many others.

The relationship between art and politics is very clear in the lives of these women. Carving as a Jamaican for Jamaica was a political act. Legitimizing the Jamaican dialect was a political act; and creating Trinidadian dance also a political act. Beryl McBurnie has said that "Art is politics," and this is precisely because art is bound up with values and aesthetics. That the Jamaican language was beautiful was a revolutionary idea at a time when the valued language was the "King's english", and finding and expressing the African roots in dance in Trinidad, a radical act, at a time when the foxtrot and the scottish reel were the "real" dances.

Perhaps the most radical artist was Calypso Rose. Sculpting, dancing, painting and writing poetry were permitted activities for women if not totally approved by society. A female in calypso was rare and certainly not condoned, but Rose's head was so full of calypso that she went ahead and risked disapproval. Rose's political act then was to create a legitimate place for women in calypso. Many women have criticised Rose, saying that her calypsos do not reflect a real departure from the calypsos men wrote. It is felt that Singing Francine, with her calypso "Run Away", is more of a feminist calypsonian. This may be true, but Calypso Rose did introduce women's sexual feelings and their view of male infidelity in the calypso "Wha she go do". And Calypso Rose's presence made it more possible for Singing Francine and others. It was Calypso Rose who broke ground by winning all the calypso titles in Trinidad that were traditionally won only by men.

It is hoped that the reader will see the strength, tenaciousness and belief in self, and in the culture of the region, that these women had. It was critically important to the development of indigenous culture that these women stayed and struggled. Without them these countries would not be as culturally rich as they are today.

Louise Bennett
"Miss Lou"

September 7, 1919
Dialect Poet and Comedienne
Jamaica

Meme, her grandmother, called her "Bibs"; everyone in Jamaica calls her "Miss Lou"; her name is Louise Bennett. She was born in Kingston, Jamaica, on the seventh day of September, 1919. She was an only child, her mother was a seamstress and her father a businessman, Bennett the baker, who died when she was seven years old. Her grandmother Meme was her favourite. She loved the warm, secure feeling of being rocked in her lap and she was devoted to her Meme as many children are to their grandparents. When Meme wanted to go to the country to die, "Bibs" went with her:

> I remember the day when the car came, and she said I was to go with her. She used to love me. And I loved that old lady, oh my gosh! When she died it was one of the saddest, saddest times in my life. I can remember that I was a little girl and how I wept.

These ties to relatives and adults were commonplace in Miss Lou's youth. She was surrounded by loving, caring people.

> This is the way I grew up. Beloved, when I tell you beloved, I just found a lot of love around me.

Her childhood, although marked by the deaths of her father and Meme, was a happy one. She was an extroverted child who had a quick mind, an ear for sounds and a knack for recitation and performance. These qualities made her popular. She was always making up stories on the teacher, coining phrases, poems, songs and rhymes. She got into many scrapes and had her share of licks but she remained irrepressible. She was never shy and she loved to perform. All her performances were based on what she observed in the people around her, particularly adults. As a child, she wrestled with the double messages around her. The people she loved, and who loved her, had dinkyninnies, sang folk songs, had wakes, and pocomanias and spoke in dialect. Yet at school you were supposed to recite English poems, speak "correctly" and write with "proper" grammar. The people she loved were different from the person she was being schooled to become. This was not true just for herself, but true for all the other children. When she began to create her dialect poems and recite them, she was in an unconscious way legitimizing herself and her friends. They listened to her not only because she was creative, funny and a good performer, but because in expressing the humour, beauty and love around her, she was speaking not only for herself, but for them too. She spoke what they knew and understood. What was Jamaican and black also belonged on centre stage.

When I used to go to school the folklore was very strong. You would hear people singing the folksong on the streets. The first time I heard a whole lot of them was when Meme died at the Dinkyninny. Dinkyninny is a function that they have to cheer up the family of a dead person. They would sing and dance. A lot of families don't allow "Dinky" in their yard, because, you see, anything black was bad.

Anything that came out of slavery that was a tradition of the black people was not good. But the people were never phased, if you don't have it in your yard, then they will have it in another yard. As a child I couldn't understand why these songs were ostracised or disparaged.

Seeing these cultural expressions prevail, despite restrictions to their very existence, was an important lesson in her early life. She appeared in all sorts of school plays and concerts. When she was nine years old she appeared in one particular play that was so successful that it was put on at other venues with special requests for her performance. At that time a man by the name of Cupidon saw Bibs. He was reported to be the greatest comedian in Jamaica. He was so impressed that he asked Bibs' mother to allow her to appear in a play. Her mother refused, saying that she was too young. Cupidon died in the 1940s. All throughout school Miss Lou performed and attracted many outsiders who came to see her performances, including Eric Coverly. He wanted her to perform in one of his Christmas shows and asked her mother's permission, which was given. It was her first professional performance; she was sixteen years old. She received one guinea (about five dollars). Much later she married Eric Coverly.

Miss Lou's ambition was always to write. At first she wrote poems, but they were in standard English, not in the dialect form for which she is now famous. Her first dialect poem was written when she was fourteen years old.

The first one. I can always remember the first dialect poem I wrote. I was in high school and I was going to what we call 'movies theatre' and you paid nine pence and you went to matinee. So now any day we come home from school early and we have matinee money, we could dress up in we clothes and we go pan tram car and we go to cross roads. Well my dear one day I was dressed and waiting on a tram car. This car was a market tram, it wasn't really a market car. The

market people sat at the back with their baskets, so they cannot sit in front, so they are very annoyed when anybody come
and sit in the back — that is anybody who is not a market
person. When I was on the tram that day, there were no seats
in front, so I decided to go in the back. Well I was fourteen
and portly and was dressed up so I didn't look like a fourteen
year old. So one woman said to another woman,
'Pread out youself, one dress woman a come. Pread out.'
And me dear everybody start pread dem apron all over de
seat dem. And I wrote the first set on this, when I went home
I wrote it. The next day I tried it out in school and it sweet
them.

This was the start of her writing career, but most importantly,
she began to write material which she herself performed. They
were always based on her own experiences, things she observed
or heard.

Then I started to write and I realized more and more that this
is what I should do because this is what I understand and
this is what the people were saying. More was being said in
that language than in any other thing and nobody was listening to them.

Her writing and performing careers were now inextricably
linked. She belonged to youth groups, church groups and the
Y.W.C.A., these were the main arenas for her performances. Still
she was determined to make it as a writer and went almost daily
to the Jamaica Gleaner, the City newspaper, seeking to have her
poems published, but with no success.

Soon one of her performances gained her a radio spot. Following her radio performance, she was asked to read some of her
poems at a private dinner party the next evening. A guest at this
party was the managing director of the Gleaner where she had
been taking her writing repeatedly. He said, "Why don't you bring
some of your work in tomorrow morning." She said "Certainly
I will." She said nothing about seeing him previously. When she
left the next morning to meet with him, her mother said
"Whatever he offers you take it. This will be your chance to see
how well you can do."

He offered her a weekly column in the Sunday Gleaner. Her
pay was half a guinea, approximately two dollars and fifty cents.

The column grew immensely popular.

> I used to write on very topical things, on whatever was hap-
> pening. It was in the Sunday Gleaner, and people would just
> buy the Sunday Gleaner to read it. People would say to me on
> the street, "I looking for you in the Sunday Gleaner."

She became Miss Lou, a national figure. As the popularity of
her work grew, she became conscious of the legitimacy and importance of what she was doing. She started to study the Jamaican
dialect in earnest and to gather stories and sayings and other
expressions of the folk culture. She was constantly being invited
to village festivals where people not only recited her poetry, but
performed and interpreted her poems. She started a movement
that took on a life of its own.

Although she was a natural and skilled dramatist on her own,
she soon realized she needed additional skills and exposure. She
was encouraged to apply for a British Council Scholarship. One
evening she was performing at a function which was attended
by a high-ranking official of the British Council. A week later she
received a telegram from England offering her a scholarship to
the Royal Academy of Dramatic Arts.

The Royal Academy of Dramatic Arts is a highly prestigious institution. Only the very talented are accepted to study at this
academy and only after competitive auditions. Miss Lou arrived
at the Academy. It was her first time abroad and she was determined to succeed. The room was filled with people and she was
standing there trying to get her bearings and to understand what
she was supposed to do. A woman came into the room and said,
"Numbers one to ten follow me."

> Dem no give me no number and she calling numbers and I
> getting vexer and vexer now you know. "Numbers ten to
> twenty!" De room a get empty and empty. Me say dem people
> here very bad. Dem don't want no black people a dem yard.
> Next thing, the woman come back and said, "Number thirty-
> three!" No answer. "Number thirty-three!" No answer.
> "Number thirty-three!" No answer.
>
> I jump up and I gone wid her. Next thing I know I am on the
> stage and there is a flood-light on my face. I hear a voice say,
> "Number thirty-three will you do something for diction?"

I said slowly, "you are a very funny old gentleman and very long and skinny." (Much laughter, she did not know that she was looking at a man who fitted this description exactly.)

"Do something for dramatic expression."

I said I didn't know I had to do something, but I'll do something in Jamaican dialect. This is about a Jamaican boy who came back from America and his mother is very upset with him because he doesn't have an accent. I did it slowly. After I finished he said,

"Do another."

I said I'll do a scene. It is a court scene and I will play all the characters in the court. I did this court scene and when I finish, he said,

"Thank you number thirty-three."

I ended up back in the same room I started from. Well the woman come back and she reel off a whole heap a number and said,

"You may go home."

Me sit down there and she sendin home everybody but she not sendin me. Finally she said, "Number thiry-three follow me." She took me aside and said, "You have passed on a scholarship."

I said, "But I am here on a Jamaica British Council scholarship."

"Jamaica?"

Me dear it turn out I was in de wrong room, I was no number thirty-three. Number thirty-three had mumps.

Miss Lou not only had a scholarship to attend the academy but having gotten there she auditioned and won a scholarship on her own merit, error that it was. She did what she knew best, Jamaican dialect, and she did it in the highest seat of drama in England.

Of course we must learn English but I think that Jamaican people have more to say in their language than in English. It is the language of the country. It is three hundred years we been talking it. It is not a corruption of anything. It is, mind you, a regional dialect because it belongs to an island, we can't expect everybody to understand it. After all English only start pon a little island over there and we still learn it.

Louise Bennett's life has been full of awards, from a little book of Claude McKay's Poems given to her by Miss Biggs in school, to the Musgrave Gold Medal of Jamaica. The awards, the books, the poems, the articles are too numerous to mention. She has appeared on film, been written about, talked about and interviewed. She has taught and performed in England and in the Caribbean. 1986 marked her 50th year as a performer, an event celebrated in Gordon Town her home, and in England and North America.

Her eyes reflect the light and laughter that her artistry evokes. She has seen the Jamaica that she knew and loved at first disparaged and then take centre stage. Now the beauty and integrity in the language and culture of the Jamaican people is a force because Louise Bennett was among the first to stand up for it. In her book *Jamaica Labrish*, Miss Lou has a poem called "Him Deh Yah." It is a poem about the great black actor, Paul Robeson, who was an outspoken advocate for racial equality at a time when this was dangerous for a black man. Paul Robeson visited Jamaica in 1948 and the poem was written in commemoration of his visit. Some of the sentiments she expressed in this poem are today applicable to Miss Lou.

> An doah de voice like it dah —
> come out o' him mout part,
> it soun to we like him dah —
> coax de song out o' him heart.
>
> An wen him done de clappin an
> De cheerin' from the crowd!

McArtha Lewis

Calypso Rose
Trinidad and Tobago
April 27, 1940

One Sunday morning McArtha's aunt sent her to the market to buy some pork. She was standing in line and all of a sudden,

> this young fellow came and snatched this lady glasses right off her eyes and started to run. People started to bawl thief! thief! murder! thief! and people started to run the guy through the market, and I said, Oh Good, look at that. I went home now and I started telling my aunt what took place in

that market and I wrote a calypso that same Sunday. It was my
first Calypso — Glass Thief...

Well Tobagonian boys, Tobagonian boys
Stay in your island and raise you fowl
Jane went to de market to buy a piece of ice
and a fellow snatch de glasses from off she eyes.

This calypso was written in 1955. The next year Dr. Eric Williams
went to Tobago to celebrate his election. The entertainment was
impromptu; members of the audience performed whatever they
wanted. McArtha and her sister were in the audience. She said
to her sister, "I goin up and sing my calypso" her sister said, "go,
go man." McArtha went on stage and sang her calypso, 'Glass
Thief.' She brought the house down. Everyone stood up and
cheered. The strength of her voice was striking and the quality
of her calypso was impressive. Afterwards Prime Minister Eric
Williams shook her hand and said, "You should really be in
Trinidad singing calypso. You are fantastic." He then had a voucher
for five dollars made out to her. This was the first payment she
received for singing calypso. At the age of fifteen, she became
a professional calypsonian. Like many other children in the Caribbean she too was raised by a person other than her mother. Her
aunt from Barataria came to take one of the children to live with
her in Trinidad. McArtha's mother made them all line up so her
aunt could choose. She chose McArtha who was shy and quiet.
Life in Trinidad was exciting, and although she would go back
to Tobago for holidays, she still missed her brothers and sisters.
She liked her new life though, because the food was good and
going to school was easy.

Her first ambition was to be a nurse. Later, she wanted to be
a policewoman. She finally decided on becoming a calypsonian.
She said to her aunt:

Tanty I think I goin write calypso and sing.

Her aunt did not like it at all. She thought that the girl was mad
and forbade her to have anything to do with calypso. Her father,
a Baptist Minister, was outraged. No nice Christian girl at that
time would be so brazen even to think of calypso as a field of
activity. Everyone was against it — except McArtha. It was
something she loved, it was something she was good at, and it

was something that gave her recognition.

In the mid-1950's, calypso was making the transition from being perceived as rude lower-class songs to a powerful and widely recognized art form. It was the era of Bomber, Fighter and Spoiler. Sparrow was just beginning to make his name. It was an entirely male-dominated field and certainly not an avenue for young women. Painting, dancing, singing (in the European tradition), writing and even acting were somewhat accepted as pursuits for women, but certainly not calypso.

The presence of women in calypso goes back to its roots when it was called kaiso. Originally calypso started as impromptu songs of praise or derision. During the 1840's in St. Lucia, there were singing groups who would perform in this genre. The most important person was the female singer or the 'chanterelle.' She would compose the 'belair' which was a song of satire or praise. In his book, The Trinidad Carnival, Errol Hill notes that these "native improvisatoris were all women." Piti Belle Lily, Alice Sugar, Mossie Millie, Ocean Lizzie, Sybil Steele, Darling Dan and Ling Mama are just a few names on a very long list of women in calypso legend. Perhaps the most notorious of all the women was Bodicea. She was said to have "a beautiful voice, a masculine face and was a wizard at extemporaneous verses. Her life was devoted to three things — singing, drinking and fighting." After the emancipation of the slaves, women began to emulate the English model of womanhood. In order to be a respectable woman, you got married, stayed at home and raised children. Although this was not in reality possible for most Caribbean women, it was a very highly-esteemed state. Women in calypso slowly faded into a thing of the past. By the time McArtha wanted to be a calypsonian, there was only one woman calypsonian of note. Her name was Madam Iree. McArtha was undaunted by the pressure from her family and society. She started frequenting Uncle Tom's Calypso Tent on Nelson Street. All the established calypsonians sang there — Bomber, Fighter, and Spoiler, but most supportive was Spoiler. He gave her the name Cruso Kid in the early days. It was with this name that she traveled with a roving group of calypsonians who would perform in different villages on weekends. In 1960, the manager of this roving calypso brigade decided that Cruso

Kid was not the right name for her. He chose instead the name
of Calypso Rose.

In these early days of Rose's career, she was often the target
of snide remarks.

> look at she na, she want go up dey and sing wid man, why
> she don't go and look for something else to do.
> I didn't mind, I had in mind that I would be the greatest
> female calypsonian ever, and that I would capture every
> Calypso crown.

Rose's arrival on the calypso scene brought a female perspective
to the topics written about and sung in calypso. It has been
argued that calypsos often denigrated women. The lyrics of many
calypsos have portrayed women as untrustworthy, interested only
in marriage and controlling men, and as objects to be assaulted
both sexually and physically. Many of Rose's calypsos portrayed
women in an assertive and forthright manner. One example is
her calypso 'What She Go Do'.

> I could understand why a woman must have a outside man
> I could understand why a woman must have a outside man
> A man does want to run like rat
> And have his wife to abide by that
> And every night he is having a ball
> And when he reach home he aint kissing the wife at all.

Rose has said that,

> Many of my calypsos were written from stories that women
> themselves told me. I try to write about the sufferings of
> women as much as I can. When I first started out it was the
> women who criticized me most. Now look how time change
> eh. Women's clubs and so invite me to speak. When my
> calypsos don't make a hit it is as if I am lettin them down.

It was unusual to have women speaking for themselves openly
in calypso. Many women feel that Rose as a general rule did not
depart significantly from what men wrote about women because
she sang and wrote about sex openly. Although there is some
truth in this statement, Rose was in a man's world and it was in
this world that she succeeded. Rose was simply talking about
women's feelings.

At one point she was accused of being the chief purveyor of smut. This has been a criticism of calypso and calypsonians historically.

In 1963, Rose made calypso history by entering the Tobago Calypso King Competition and winning. The win qualified her to enter the National Calypso King Competition. At this point she began traveling, her first tour being with Sparrow's group. They went to the Virgin Islands where she became the first female to win the calypso competition there. During Carnival time she worked in Fighter's tent. In those days calypsonians singing in a tent with major name like Fighter were called helpers. Helpers were not given a salary but were paid according to the evening's financial success. By 1966 she was receiving $100.00 a week for the carnival season. This was because she had a monumental hit called "Fire! Fire!" which made her known throughout the Caribbean. Along with "Fire! Fire!" she had recorded another tune called "A Man is A Man." These calypsos were so popular that the public requested them again in 1967. It was the first time in Calypso history that a record was requested to be sung for two consecutive years.

She began entering the national competition and was placing either second or third. Now there was a new category, the calypso Queen competition. This she won from 1974 for five consecutive years. Her calypso 'Give me more tempo' won the road march in 1977. By 1978 she had captured every crown in calypso. She had won the Calypso Queen Competition, was the first woman to win the Road March title and finally the first woman to win the National Monarch title in 1978.

While she was backstage after her performance for the title in 1978, someone told her that she had won the National Monarch Title. She could not believe it.

> No man all you jokin.
> 'Yes, yes you win de crown.'
> I didn't believe it until the Chairman shook my hand. I was very proud. I was happy because I had achieved what I wanted — I won every crown in calypso.

Although women were very much involved in the creation of the calypso as an art form, their presence eroded over time.

Calypso Rose's presence in the 1950's returned women to this art form. Even though there are still relatively few women in calypso the precedent has been set. She is an artist whose contribution to calypso has been historic.

> I didn't get it at all easy in this career. I made a tune called 'I am what I am.' I consider this tune to be my greatest composition. I wrote it to coincide with all the awards and all the suffering and all the pain I pass through.
>
> Don't try to change my name
> Don't try to take away my fame
> I suffer long from where I came from
> So don't try to chain me down.
> It was a heavy load
> And a rugged road
> To walk
> Night and day
> So I pray, and pray and pray
> On Christ the solid rock I stand
> I am, what I am.

Edna Manley

February 28, 1900 — February 10, 1987
Sculptor
Jamaica

Edna Manley walked to school every day, with her dog Mike.

> He went to school with me every day. We walked nearly two
> miles to school or more and this dog would go up to a cer-
> tain spot on the road, and I would say "home now Mike" and
> he would go home. And then when it got to the time that I
> was due to return home from school my mother would say
> "Get Edna" and he would come and wait for me. Oh it was
> magic in Cornwall.

Edna lived in Cornwall until she was sixteen, but she was born in Hampshire, England on February 28, 1900. Her childhood was influenced by her being the middle child of nine children, by her love for animals and a thirst for freedom.

> I would run away from the house at 6 o'clock in the morning and not come home until 7 o'clock at night, out on the moors, down by the sea with nothing particularly to eat. My sisters were so mad because they said I did it to avoid housework. I just don't know why I did it and I had such temper tantrums. I think the slightest thing I thought was un- just whether to me or anybody else, that was part of it. And I think it was a sense of frustration. I wanted to be alone, and as a child I could not stand so many in the family. I remember this quite clearly.

This intense child grew up to be a world renowned sculptor, and the force behind the Jamaican Art Movement. Her husband was the first Premier of Jamaica and her son a Prime Minister. Her achievements in the field of sculpture and in the history of art in Jamaica are legend. Her relationship with her husband Norman Manley reads like an epic romance.

Her father was an Englishman, a pastor who lived in Jamaica and her mother was a Jamaican. They returned to England after their first two children were born. When Edna was nine years old her family moved to Cornwall. Her father's death shortly thereafter affected her deeply. Cornwall itself to her was stun- ning; the sea and the moors captivated her.

> And of course it was in Cornwall in a magic summer that I met my husband.

She was fourteen and he was her cousin. He had come to England to attend Oxford. It was not love at first sight. She found his first visit an inconvenience.

> I just thought he'd come there to make us have to be tidy for supper or something. I was out jumping hayricks and you know to have to come because Norman was coming, I didn't think that was fair.

Over a period of seven years they fell in love: when she was twenty-one they finally married. During this time she went to London to art school, which proved a frustrating experience.

She must have attended at least four different art schools before finding a teacher that impressed her.

> I couldn't stand the method of teaching art, you see. I just couldn't. You had to draw from antiques and draw perfectly and work from still life and I just didn't think that was art as far as I was concerned at all. And I was right because I walked and walked and walked and I found a marvelous teacher at St. Martin who understood me and I could understand his type of discipline. I stayed with him and I always felt that he really believed in me. He would come at 9 o'clock and I would be there. And I'd stay until 11 at night if I could get the chance. His name was McCrossen. He was very Scotch and he used to say, "don't work in the round, look for the planes, lassie, look for the planes." I adored him, he was a bit like the rocks of Cornwall.

McCrossen was the first major influence on her art. She did not suddenly decide that she wanted to be an artist, it was something she did all along. "Oh I was always drawing, always animals, horses and dogs." She finished up at St. Martin's, had her first baby and then left for Jamaica at the age of 22.

She arrived in Jamaica, a wife, a mother and a person with the eye and senses of an artist.

> When the boat parked, if I may put it that way, there was a fantastic sky, flaming, reflected in the harbour. I thought, ah you know, this is it. A friend met us with a car and we were driving up Orange Street and there was a marvelous looking young, very black, very straight young woman, about eighteen and she was striding, and this was what I had been looking for, people who really walked. She had on her head a sewing machine, and it was at a forty-five degree angle and every now and then she would move and catch her balance. And I could nearly jump out the car I was so excited. This movement you didn't get in England at all.

As Norman worked at establishing his career as a lawyer, Edna attempted to settle down with the baby and to sculpting. She was an artist who exercised her options. The movement, the colour and the richness of Jamaica dazzled her. The same spirit that had made her take off for the moors in Cornwall and not come home till nightfall made her sit for hours in the market place drinking in the scenery. She shocked everyone by this. A lady of "good" family did not sit on a wall in the market place, particularly if she were wearing an orange dress. It was from this experience that she made her first carving called The Beadseller. This is an historic piece as it is the first Jamaican sculpture that Edna Manley did. Like many of her other works it is in the National Gallery of Jamaica. When she carved The Beadseller, she lived in Mandeville.

> Well I turned Mandeville upside down, they thought I was something out of a book. I wore an orange jumper and then I went out and sat on the market wall and watched the market women coming in. I was fascinated, and this woman was sitting selling these strings of beads and from that the beadseller came.

A year later her second son Michael was born. The reality of life in Jamaica in the 1920s had begun to have its effect. She was an artist, living in an environment in which the artist was marginal. She needed people to talk to, to understand her work, to appreciate her work. She needed a context and there was none. Yet she continued to sculpt.

> It was a very lonely life for an artist and I struggled on and people who saw the work ridiculed it. They made me feel awful and I smashed something because of what somebody said, but slowly I fought through and I went on exhibiting in England. I was a member or the Society of Women Artists, I was a member of the London group and I continued to exhibit.

It is important that an artist work and exhibit. There were no exhibitions in Jamaica and her only audience was in England. Her husband was engrossed in his career, which increased her sense of loneliness. The experience of coming to a new country and attempting to establish herself as an artist was a harsh and painful experience to the vulnerable young Edna. She and her baby returned to England in 1923. She soon realized that England was not for her; she wanted to be with her husband and in Jamaica and it was not long before she returned. Her exhibitions abroad gave her recognition as a sculptor; in 1931 she and a fellow artist Koren dor Harootian had their own exhibition, her first in Jamaica.

> We made a point of not going to the opening, leaving them

with it and sitting down at the end of the pier and cooling our feet in the water.

In 1931, she was established enough to have her first one-woman show in England. By that time, her husband had already established himself as a brilliant lawyer and had launched into politics. When she returned from England she was caught up in this new era of political consciousness.

> By the time I came back, there was self-government. Nationalism had come. Then I made a decision that I would not exhibit abroad any more. It was a concrete decision, that such as I had a talent I was going to exhibit here. I was going to set a pattern and take the knocks. I felt that anything else would have been purely escapist, it wouldn't have been any value to me. I was so totally caught up with this.

This decision was critical not only to Edna Manley's life and art but to the history of art in Jamaica. There were other writers, poets and painters who were also struggling; together they evolved into an art movement that was truly Jamaican. The criteria for art were being questioned. What was the value of Jamaicans writing about snow and apple trees when they had never seen them? Why were they not writing about breadfruit and plantain and ackee?

> It was at that time that we had the great showdown with ourselves. We had some good poets — and they were writing about snow and daffodils and things they'd never seen and so we would have these terrific quarrels and tear up each other's works. It must be rooted in Jamaica, or at least the Caribbean, the climate of it, the fauna, the mountains.

It was in this vein that the Jamaican Art Movement progressed. Edna, having known the loneliness and isolation herself, was able to encourage and guide many young artists. She started *Focus,* a literary and political publication which became a forum for many young writers.

Her greatest personal encouragement came with the purchase of her sculpture "Negro Aroused" in 1937. The piece was symbolic of the times and the wave of nationalism that was spreading across the country. It was bought by public subscription for 100 Pounds.

> It was tremendously important to me and I was touched to
> tears over it. If I had sold it in England it wouldn't have had
> the same effect but my people wanted it, my people had
> subscribed. This was what mattered.

These acts of recognition, in the press in Jamaica and in the
purchase of her art, were symbolic in the creation of a tradition
of art in Jamaica. It gave her encouragement and eased the
loneliness. Throughout all of this her main support was Norman
Manley. He loved the arts and he would provide both the encouragement and criticism that were so essential. They were both
outstanding people with special gifts and in the lean years, just
after returning to Jamaica, they often had only each other for
stimulating conversation.

> I'm the luckiest person you see because any other kind of
> man, and I wouldn't have done anything. I would have just
> frittered myself away, but he had no respect for people if they
> had taken on work and didn't put the whole of themselves
> into it. He found my work a release and we would have
> tremendous discussions about it and in a way we stimulated
> each other, we kept each other alive.

Norman became Premier in 1955 and her role as the premier's
wife so consumed her time that she gave up sculpting for seven
years. She missed it, but these years were of great value to her.
"I traveled every nook and cranny of Jamaica and saw things and
absorbed them: I learned a lot."

Both her son Michael Manley and her husband Norman chose
politics as their spheres. She herself chose art, but her art was
political and in a way she too was political. Carving as a Jamaican
for Jamaica was a political act. The push to discover Jamaica and
to discover the beauty of the black race and the Jamaican way
of life was political. Some people argue that art should be for
its own sake and should be free of politics. Others argue that
all art is political: that even the drawing of a flower makes a
political statement, because it reflects the class, values, nationality
and aesthetics of the artist and her view of the world. Edna
Manley's art was political because she insisted that Jamaican
artists reflect Jamaica and Jamaican values.

Norman Manley died in 1969. "After Norman died, the thing
that saved me was my art."

Edna Manley was a striking woman, slim and statuesque. She had a deep clear voice that enveloped you rather than overwhelmed you. She dressed with flair and had a certain puckishness about her. She decided in 1975 to give up sculpting as it was too taxing for her. She took up painting.

The volume on her art alone is yet to be written. Her life up until 1938 has already been documented in the book Edna Manley, The Private Years, 1900-1938. She was a person who was able to maintain her own identity and did not live in the shadow of her famous husband.

Edna Manley died on February 10, 1987, a few weeks short of her 87th birthday. She was passionately Jamaican. When she was asked, "What do you think has been your most significant contribution to Jamaica?", her reply was no different from Miss Tiny the higgler;

"Loving it."

Beryl McBurnie

Trinidad and Tobago
Mother of Caribbean Dance
November 2, 1917

Consciously or otherwise, our West Indian peoples have all been touched by McBurnie and the Little Carib. But her commitment to the development of a West Indian consciousness, for all its intensity, has not been narrowly chauvinistic. In the tradition of the liberated intellectual she has shown that the establishment of cultural identity carries with it the respect for universality of human endeavour and behaviour. She is among the first of a small but increasing band of West Indian artists who, through their great talents, have given the West Indies its soul.

This was part of the proclamation written for Beryl McBurnie when she was given an honourary doctorate by the University of the West Indies in 1976 for her contribution to dance, music and folklore. She has received many awards and accolades throughout her life, among them the Golden Arrow Crown from Guyana in 1966 and the Humming Bird Gold Medal of Honour from Trinidad and Tobago in 1969. She was among the six artists in the Caribbean honoured at Carifesta in Barbados in 1981, and was one of three Black woman (Katherine Dunham and Pearl Primus being the other two) honored by the Alvin Ailey Dance Company in New York in 1978.

Her life has been one of total dedication to dance, the folk dance of Trinidad and Tobago and the Caribbean. She was born on November 2, 1917 in Woodbrook, Trinidad in the house that later became the Little Carib Theatre. She was the first of four children; her father was a printer and her mother a singer. Her first memory as a performer was as a little girl dancing on the gallery when her grandfather, William Rollock, a musician, would rehearse his band at the house. Most of all she remembered the affection in her relationship with her grandfather, the band leader.

> Every morning I used to climb up on his chair and peep into his cup. He used to leave a little coffee for me. So every morning I would look into the cup and see the coffee that grandpa left for me — to me that was his love.

She came from a family of performers and would have her own performances in her mother's drawing room.

She attended Tranquility School and was first taught dance by Ms. Fraser. After finishing high school she went to teacher's training college and then left for Columbia University in 1938. During her adolescence and childhood the main entertainment was live performance. There was no television or radio. Beryl therefore formed a little group who would perform at her house. No one came to the very first show she organized because of rain, but Beryl continued with her group of friends and as she grew older her passion for dance grew. She danced as often as she could and developed her music and voice skills as well. She became interested in the folk dances of Trinidad and Tobago and was encouraged by Andrew Carr, a very distinguished Trinidadian folklorist of the times.

Trinidad at that time could not provide Beryl McBurnie with opportunities for growth in her art. Her interest in the folk culture was frowned upon — it was an interest in slavery and people wanted to separate themselves from this. This discouragement led her to New York where she studied with Martha Graham. As La Belle Rosette (her theatrical name), she became an enormously successful dancer. She had many performances in New York and her dancing was so passionate and colourful that one observer described her as "legend fire". The famous dancer Katherine Dunham, who was known for her African and Caribbean dance rhythms, was greatly influenced by her work with Beryl McBurnie.

Molly Ahye, in *Cradle of Caribbean Dance,* , notes that

> The first person to promote primitive and Caribbean dancing was not Katherine Dunham but Beryl McBurnie, who was originally from Trinidad. I am told that Dunham took lessons when she came to New York City from Chicago. Beryl McBurnie left New York after many people began to copy her dances and is now heading the "Little Carib". [1]

She returned in 1940 and put on her first official dance concert called "A Trip Through the Tropics" which was so successful that it ran for several days. From 1942 to 1945 she worked with a highly talented group of dancers called the Beryl McBurnie Dance Troupe with Boscoe Holder as its mainstay in Trinidad, she continued to work abroad demonstrating Caribbean dance at many colleges in the U.S. and did research in South America and Trinidad on the origins of Caribbean dance. In 1947, after having done her research, she returned to Trinidad to work in earnest with a group called the Little Carib Dance Company.

The first order of business was a place to perform. Thanks to Clara Rollock, The Little Carib became possible.

> My Aunt Clara Rollock, my mother's sister, changed the ownership of the property where the Carib is to give it to us.

But this house where Beryl McBurnie was born needed to be made into a theatre, a little intimate local theatre for artists to dance and perform. Beryl was inspired to call it the Little Carib after one of her trips to South America.

> I went on a field trip of research in South America and in Cayenne I saw a little place that was so charming to make a little intimate theatre, and I drew it on the spot, and brought it back to an architect called Aldwyn Beckles, and he inter-

preted it to mean — what you saw there on White street in the early days: the first Little Carib Theatre.[2]

Beryl McBurnie's life cannot be fully appreciated unless one understands the state of the arts at the time in Trinidad. Woodbrook, the community in which she lived was bent on being very English. What happened at funerals and at wakes of Black people and the dances of the hispanic creoles was to be kept as far away from Woodbrook as possible. This was an association with slavery, a step back, not a step forward. And yet, Beryl was fascinated with these folk cultures. Imagine the audacity of this behaviour. What she was doing in the 1930's and 40's was seen by many as negative to the Black race which in Trinidad and in other areas of colonization was trying to mimic the white race. It was in this environment that she wanted to legitimize folk dance in Trinidad.

> They laugh at me, they run me. When I tried to bring the Parang, a Scottish woman said, we don't want national dance here. The rhythm is so infectious, so infectious. They don't want anything black. A lot of people thought it was politics but it was pride.

There was no money, only a struggling art, no place to dance not even the steelband had been established yet. And so Beryl McBurnie had to slowly give up the dance and work for a place for the dance. She enlisted the support of many influential people and with their help, the little Carib was built. She had to constantly solicit. "My dear, the only person I didn't beg was the devil himself."

Finally, in February 1948, the Little Carib Theatre was formally opened. This was an important moment in the history of Trinidad and Tobago, for the nation now had a symbolic place to develop its cultural identity. Many important people were at this opening; among them was Audrey Jeffers and Dr. Eric Williams. Beryl McBurnie recalled this as the most important moment in her career.

> Because he came, Paul Robeson came and he was so moved that he got up and said so. I will never forget that night. Oh it was electric, oh just look at me, goose bumps just remembering. Oh what a voice, what a beautiful man. He congratulated me and then recited the poem Freedom Train.[3]

Paul Robeson had stopped in Trinidad during his tour of the Caribbean in 1948. He had intended to stay only a few minutes on his visit to the Little Carib that evening, but he was so captivated by the dance program that he stayed on and laid the foundation stone with Audrey Jeffers. In his speech afterwards he said that "the encouragement of West Indian art forms being performed by Beryl McBurnie was as significant a thing as he had ever come upon in his life."[4]

What was it that made Beryl McBurnie creative and original? Certainly one contributing factor was her ability to see the beauty and drama of the everyday movements and rituals of the Trinidadian.

> Theatre is my first love. I did the drama first before dancing. As a young child I did plays and later tried the dances of Trinidad and Tobago. Our first dances were interpreted from American dances. And up came Ms. Fraser at Tranquility School and she teaches us the scottish reel and the street cries of London. So I put that to Trinidad.
>
> In London it was Strawberries!
> Gooseberries!
> Cockles! Cockles!
>
> And Trinidad now it was
> Ice! Ice!!!
> Hot ice!, Cold Ice! Ice Ice!!
> Zabocas!
> Zah B O CAAS!!!
>
> You see it has its own rhythm listen to it, say it. And I built a whole harmony from our street cries.

In Ahye's *Cradle of Caribbean Dance*, Holly Betaudier remembered that Beryl McBurnie used the music of Bach and during improvisation period she would ask the students to volunteer movements from everyday life. She focused attention on the various occupations, especially of the rural folk, and transposed them into dance movements using the music of Bach. Progressing from this she would then take them through drum rhythms and exercises based on the movements of various folk dances.[5]

It was this ability to see the relationship of Bach to the Trinidad folk movement and the street cries of London to the street cries of Trinidad that made Beryl's work exciting and original. But what was critical was her understanding of the rhythm of Trinidad and Tobago.

> The basic rhythm of our culture is syncopated, a calypso rhythm and if you are building a culture you must come back to the ritual. The whole spirit of the country is calypso. The folk rhythm is national, cultural — the child must be exposed to both the classical and our own folk rhythms.

Beryl McBurnie was able to choreograph from a knowledge of both classical western music and dance and her own folk music and dance. She legitimized the dance of Trinidad and Tobago and of the Caribbean by showing that the movements of the common folk were as beautiful as Bach and ballet; and moreover, they also had their own cultural tradition.

This creativity was her first contribution. Next was the creation of the Little Carib Theatre. Her other contributions range from teaching and molding many talented dancers, to promoting the steelband, to starting a training theatre, to introducing folk dance to the school system and choreographing a dance with 2,000 school children for the Queen's visit to Trinidad and Tobago. From 1948 to 1958, Beryl McBurnie received a great deal of recognition, but around 1960 the dance movement entered a new era. Many talented dancers left for opportunities abroad and other dance groups were formed. For those without the stamina and resilience of Beryl McBurnie, remaining in Trinidad as a dancer was extremely limiting. Outside of a few groups, Beryl McBurnie and the Little Carib, there was no scope. The promise of the fifties to support a national theatre was not fulfilled; some of her dances were not well received and as her image of Mother of Caribbean dance took hold she became less involved in the theatre. She started Folk House: "a place for the children, a training theatre." This opening up of her home made her vulnerable and she was robbed a few times of very special collections of music and other memorabilia.

Also at this time, a crisis developed in the Little Carib between her and Helen Camps, who had taken on the role of manager of the theatre. Beryl McBurnie's feeling was that the folk dance was being neglected and the supporters of Helen Camps felt that

Beryl did not want to pass the leadership of the Little Carib on to others. This crisis was important for one significant reason: it was a rallying point for Trinidadians concerning the direction of art and theatre in their country. The debate was public and passionate. It marked a renaissance of the art movement of that country and at the center of it was Beryl McBurnie.

Beryl McBurnie has spent more than twenty years soliciting for the theatre. To build Folk House she used money from her gratuity and other earnings from a movie about dance in Trinidad in which she appeared. She feels disappointed that art, particularly folk dance, is not more advanced in Trinidad, that the government does not support a national theatre, that there aren't enough teachers in the schools to give the grounding in folk dance, "and that too many people are copying the styles of American dancers and choreographers."

This remarkable woman has lived a life of great rewards and sacrifices. She has traveled extensively and was so consumed by her work that she never married nor had children.

> This whole life is too hard alone. There were no men who would share me with this art. Many woman had to give up dancing if they got married. I couldn't give up the dance.

Her contribution as a pioneer artist takes on historical significance because it was a woman who was making these strides in the 1940s and 50s. Dr. Eric Williams, in his remarks on the program of that 1948 historic opening show of the Carib, said:

> Beryl McBurnie's work of which the "Little Carib" is a visible symbol, is of the utmost social significance these days ... In the first place it is a shining light to the women of the West Indies who are so heavily handicapped by their economic status and the traditional conception of the role of women in society, and on whose full participation in the future, the life of our West Indian community will depend."

What is more striking about Beryl McBurnie's contribution as a woman was her role as one of the region's leading intellectuals. She was truly "a liberated intellectual." She combined an intelligence and a political awareness at a time when such things were radical.

> When I came back from New York I worked for the United
> Front. They sent for me and questioned me. They had me
> down as a communist. Dance is my form of nationalism. They
> say it's politics. They frighten for Beryl.

So Beryl, a pioneer of dance, struggled for years politically, emotionally and aesthetically. Her contribution has been documented
and her place prominent in the history of Trinidad and Tobago.
She still struggles today in part because it is the only life she has
known. She prefers to work with children now.

> I work with children because they are not suspicious, they are
> supple and very receptive. Most of the time teaching is easy.

It has not been an easy life for Beryl McBurnie and she was
not an easy woman. She was eccentric and fanciful. She is still
today eccentric and a vibrant and fascinating woman. From her
photographs and from seeing her, one can tell that she was a
gorgeous woman. She has style and is always theatrical and intense. When she spoke of Paul Robeson she was reverent and
spoke in a whisper. Suddenly she would say something in Trinidadian dialect like "How you mean man," in three completely different inflections. Beryl McBurnie — the beautiful, scintillating
pioneer of Caribbean dance — did everything for the love of
country and the love of dance.

> Dance was my form of nationalism. A lot of people thought it
> was politics, but it was pride.

She was indeed among "the first of a small but increasing band
of West Indian artists who, through their great talents, have given
the West Indies its soul."

---

[1]Ahye, Molly, *Cradle of Caribbean Dance*, Heritage Cultures Ltd.: Trinidad and
Tobago, 1983 (p.4)
[2]Ahye, p.4.
[3]Poem by Langston Hughes
[4]Ahye, p.32
[5]Ahye, p.30

Women in Business

Women dominate certain sectors of business in the Caribbean and in other Third World countries. They not only grow food, but have established an efficient system to market their produce. The domination of women in the market place, however, has changed over time. In the last 10 years women have taken to international travel; they have gone to Puerto Rico, the Cayman Islands, Panama, Miami and Venezuela to trade and import products needed in the home country. Vendoring has become a very serious and sophisticated operation in the Caribbean.

In this section three women are profiled, each representing a different kind of business woman. Miss Tiny, the higgler from Jamaica, represents both the old and the new vendor. Her life encompasses the shift from rural to urban, and illustrates how she parlayed the marketing skills taught to her by her mother into a livelihood for herself. Olive Valmont is a business woman in the traditional meaning of the word. She is the head of one of the largest business enterprises in St. Lucia. Again she was apprenticed to her mother. Mable Tenn, the only female Director of Grace Kennedy, the Jamaican multi-national corporation, also learned business from her mother. She earned her job as Director after successfully demonstrating that she could produce high quality canned products in Jamaica. Both Olive Valmont and Mable Tenn are in business positions not traditionally held by women.

Miss Tiny is representative of large number of business women in the Caribbean, who find elastic, zippers, the small necessities that governments will not buy. In providing these everyday items these women have often been described as the back bone of their societies. Business is an increasingly important area in the development of our society and young men and young women should see it as a viable place for them.

It is expected that after reading about these women's lives that young people will look upon the vendor with renewed appreciation. It is also hoped that the few women like Ms. Valmont and Mable Tenn will be emulated for their pioneer role in business.

More importantly, it should be discerned that it was their mothers, women of another generation, who were the true pioneer business women.

Mable Tenn

June 22, 1930
Director, Grace Kennedy Company
Jamaica

This question of being Chinese. I'm second generation Chinese. We are now in third generation, and I don't look at myself so much as a Chinese but as a Jamaican. I remember going to Honolulu and the gentleman looking at me and saying:

Well, what are you?

and I said, 'Well, I am Jamaican,' and he said

But you look like Chinese.

'Of course,' I said, 'because my ancestors are Chinese.'

M able Tenn is a Jamaican woman of Chinese ancestry. Her
father was from Canton, China, and her mother was a
Jamaican-born Chinese. They were shopkeepers in St. Andrew
and Mable was born on the 22nd of June, 1930, in Kingston,
Jamaica. Mable was the first child in a family of seven children.
Although raised by her grandmother in Kingston she still had
close ties to her family. Many children in the Caribbean who are
raised by another relative are not necessarily cut off from brothers
and sisters or their parents.

Her childhood with her grandmother was very restricted; she
was not allowed to go to the movies or to date. Like most Chinese
in Jamaica, they were devout Roman Catholics. She went to Alpha
High School and, after graduation, wanted to go to university.
However, it was unusual for young women to go to university at
that time. It was very costly. Young women were encouraged to
become secretaries or were sent to learn shorthand. At eighteen,
she became a secretary in the Jamaica Credit Union League. It
was the first job for a woman who was to become the first and
only female director of the Grace Kennedy Company in Jamaica
and recipient of the Jamaica Honour of Distinction in 1980.

After emancipation in the British Caribbean in 1838, the planters
were faced with a labour problem. The slaves immediately aban-
doned the estates they despised. The idea was that the freed
slaves would stay on the plantation as paid labourers, but the
planters were unable and unwilling to pay enough to keep those
who may have been willing to stay. A system of indentured labour
was therefore devised to supply a cheap source of labour. The
labourer would come from her country to be paid on a yearly
basis. The sum of money was approximately five dollars per year
for five years and often at the end of the tenure the labourer was
offered a plot of land as an enticement to stay. Most of them
stayed. The indentured labourers came from China, India and
Portugal. They were taken primarily to Guyana, Jamaica and
Trinidad. Most of the Chinese went to Jamaica. The first record
of Chinese presence in the British Caribbean was in 1853 in
Trinidad.

Although Mable was raised by her grandmother she spent a
lot of time with her parents in St. Andrew. Her mother was the
businesswoman who knew what decisions to make and how to

conduct the business. Her father, although he worked in the business, did all the cooking and the nurturing. Her fondest memories of him were of waiting for "Pappa to come and take us to the picture show and we would be so excited because he would take us for ice cream afterwards." She remembered that her pappa gave her a little piano when she was ten years old. If her father provided nurture, it was her mother who gave her a sense of direction and her drive to achieve. Her mother was very education-conscious and insisted that all of her children go to university. Today, they are all qualified professionals. The achievement of this educational level for her brothers and sisters was something which Mable also worked and pushed for. The time she spent with her parents in the shop gave her a grounding in business. She learned the principles of profit and loss and the relationship between people and good business. She was an apt student to an exceptional teacher, her mother.

She became, in 1952, the secretary of Carlton Alexander, who is now President of Grace Kennedy. This was her first connection with one of the largest companies in Jamaica, a multi-national organization whose business of import and export has markets and bases all over the world. She was Mr. Alexander's secretary for nine years, after which she left to run her family business.

From 1959 she embarked on a series of business attempts, a grocery store, a book store, a pharmacy and finally, a canning factory. Some of these businesses she sold but she stayed with the canning factory. It had taken much of her capital and it was running at a loss for several years, but Mable Tenn was determined to make it work.

The difficulties were enormous. There were labour problems, sanitation problems, mechanical problems, accounting problems and most of all, her own lack of knowledge in the canning process. Sometimes the cans would explode and there would be spoilage. Some cans would have more, others would have less. In making the factory work, Mable Tenn became an expert in machinery. She could walk in with a mechanic, dissemble a piece of machinery and put it back together herself. This she learned painstakingly after repeated mistakes. She went in the toilets and bathrooms and cleaned them herself, showing the workers how it was to be done. There was no concept of quality control; this she had to introduce. Her task was to produce a canned product of ackee or pineapple of the same quality or standard as a canned product in the United States or Europe. Sometimes she would have to go to the farms to see why the produce was arriving damaged and so difficult to can. Slowly she reversed the factory's fortunes. It began to make quality products at a profit.

Grace Kennedy Company bought the factory at this point and she became once again an employee of Grace Kennedy since she remained manager of the factory. This did not last very long because Mable Tenn's expertise was needed in the other Grace Kennedy Factories. In 1972 she was made one of the ten directors of the company, an historic moment in the company and for women in the country. She is one of the very few women in Jamaica at this level in a company of Grace Kennedy's magnitude. This was accomplished always by hard work, but more importantly by an attitude that allotted respect and dignity to the workers.

> When I was down in the factory I used to go down there and I would actually clean the toilets and the walls, and say this is how it is to be done and you did this because it was important. You showed by example. And one of the things is, I don't talk down to people and I wouldn't ask them to do things that I wouldn't do.

Mable Tenn's struggles with the canning factory and the food process became monumental, because she would not produce an inferior product. The process of creating a canned product that could be bought anywhere was not only a struggle for herself and her own standards, but a struggle for Jamaica, for she was creating a superior Jamaican product. She canned pineapple and sweet peppers, ackee and other items grown in Jamaica. She became an expert in every phase of the business, from the fruit from the farm to the final product in the can. She knew which fruit or vegetable could be canned or grown in Jamaica for export or local market and why. It was a struggle in Jamaica, not abroad. She dealt with the labour, the produce, the machinery, the canning process, the quality standards, all within the Jamaican context. She did not leave. "I used to change that factory around like a woman changes her bedroom." This familiarity made her an undeniable asset to her country and it was because of her valiant efforts in the agro industry that she was given the Honour of Distinction in 1980.

The interest in the agro industry originated in the business sector long before it became a symbol of nationalism. The wave of Caribbean and Jamaican migration to the United Kingdom after the Second World War created a market for items from home. The Jamaican business community responded to this market, but it was done on a small scale and certainly not at the level to which Mable Tenn took her own enterprise. Suddenly, after years of hard work, she became "relevant" because the agro industry was made a priority in the national interest. Being in this position was not accomplished by knowledge alone. It was accomplished by determination, a willingness to learn, a refusal to be defeated and most of all, by the ability to lead.

Mable Tenn found that she had become a mother-like figure to the workers in her factory. Some of them even called her mama. Her style of leadership fell into the mother category, a legitimate model that is human and caring. Unfortunately, mothers are not usually viewed as leaders. Of course, an objective look at what mothers do, shows that they do, in fact, perform leadership functions. They set the standards and directions in their families, help with the realization of education and career goals, and often supply the basic necessities for their families. This leadership is called motherhood; it frequently is the only kind of female leadership that people are exposed to, be they male or female.

Mable Tenn is an articulate woman who speaks her mind and who projects fearlessness. She is always accessible and tries to see those who wish to see her. Despite her position and status she is a down-to-earth woman whose eyes sparkle with laughter.

She has never been afraid to be herself and believes firmly that it is important, no matter what a person does, to understand people.

> Everyone should be themselves and should try to understand people and not be status-conscious because if you do your job right you will get it; because I have got it without having sought it consciously or deliberately. Where you go in life depends solely on you.

This woman, director of Grace Kennedy, recipient of the Honour of Distinction, expert in the agro industry, is the daughter of a shopkeeper from St. Andrew. She never went to university, she was able to direct the events of her life by adhering to hard work and high standards.

People have to understand when you're in charge you're in charge, it doesn't matter what your status is.

"Miss Tiny"
Esmine Antoine

August 19, 1935
Higgler, Jamaica

M iss Tiny is a higgler. Everyone calls her Miss Tiny, but her real name is Esmine Antoine and she was born on the 19th of August, 1935 in St. Andrew, Jamaica. After she left primary school she became pregnant. At the time she was growing up in Jamaica, secondary school was not free and so a difficult thing for children of poor families to pursue. Leaving her three month old baby with her mother, she left for Kingston at the age of sixteen armed with one dollar and dreams of making a living for herself.

In Kingston she stayed with a friend and bought some thyme, scallion and paper bags and sold them on a little tray on Princess Street. She was accustomed to selling as she had often helped her mother who sold produce in the St. Andrew market. This was her start as a higgler in Kingston. She became a "tray girl."

> I had a hard life, a very very hard life. From I have my six children, I don't get a hundred dollars from one of them father. Me one have to shoulder dem burden. I send me son to two high school. Me daughter I send to four different high school because she never pass any exam. I say I goin to try with them because I don't want them to suffer like me suffer. And I have to school all of them. Me and me alone.

In Jamaica, almost all higglers are women. The term "higgler" originally referred to a woman who bought items wholesale from "country people" and sold mainly agricultural produce. This was different from "country people" who sold the produce that was grown by a member of their family. Today a higgler is a general term for small vendoring businesses run by women in Jamaica. The word "higgler" is used mainly in Jamaica. Higglering is, however, a common occupation for women in the Caribbean. Women run the market system in the region: they buy, sell and also produce. In the other territories, they are known as market-women, vendors, or fishwomen. It is these women who are responsible for the supply and availability of fruit, vegetables, fish and the many other items needed in the Caribbean household.

Miss Tiny has been, at one time or another, almost every type of female vendor found in the Caribbean. Most women are initiated into the business by their mothers. An apprentice higgler serves a very important function for a higgler. The higgler is a small vendor, who sells her fare either on the streets or in open spaces in the market, so she must guard her "load" against theft. The guard is usually a child, in most cases, a daughter. Miss Tiny was the guard who kept an eye on the produce, who ran errands, helped her mother carry her bundles and who sold and interacted with customers. When she went to Kingston, selling was the only profession she knew; it influenced her start as a "tray girl."

She did this type of selling for five years. At the end of each week she would take the money she made and buy things for the baby and send them to her mother in St. Andrew. Meanwhile she met a man with whom she had four children. (She had had two other children whose father had left for England.) Miss Tiny and the children's father decided to live together as a family. She did not get married. This family type is very common in the region. The legal system only recognized those children whose parents were married as having any rights. Because of this, many children were unable to inherit their father's property and mothers had no legal recourse for child support claims. Today, many countries, including Jamaica, have changed these laws which discriminate against unmarried women and their children.

Miss Tiny, like many women in the Caribbean, based her own worth on her ability to educate her children and provide them with a secure home and family.

She heard that a little shop was for rent and decided to start a business of her own. She, the children's father and the children moved into the back of the shop. Miss Tiny ran a food shop, selling fried fish and ackee. She was now twenty-one years old. However, the shop business soon ended because the owners wanted the premises for their own purposes. The relationship with the children's father slowly disintegrated and she launched into a new phase of the vendoring business. She became a fishwoman. The fish business required a great deal of planning and forethought. The small-scale fish vendors got their supplies from the large fishing boats that came into Kingston and Miss Tiny, upon learning this, supplied herself with small quantities of fish from these boats. Buying large quantities of fish required refrigeration which she did not have. Slowly she began to increase the amount she could sell until she heard that it was cheaper to buy from fishermen in the country. This entailed leaving on a truck in the evening, waiting for the boats to come in, sleeping on the beach, making the purchase and leaving by five o'clock the next morning to catch the market business.

This constant traveling is a large part of a higgler's life. The economic and psychological demand of traveling are wearing and a higgler must be tough, aggressive, vigilant and shrewd, otherwise she will simply not make it. Miss Tiny saw that her life would be simplified by two things: her own transportation and refrigeration. Her first purchase was a freezer. This allowed her to buy large quantities and made the daily trip unnecessary. After a while she was able to buy her own van which her son learned to drive. All of this took place within a span of eight years. The van alleviated many difficulties. Traveling from Kingston to the country areas in packed buses and trucks on winding rough roads with large "loads" is an exhausting and nerve-wracking experience. Although higglers become accustomed to this, it never means that it is less uncomfortable and harrowing. To be a higgler with your own transportation is quite an impressive feat. Miss Tiny was able to realise this dream. Not only was she able to buy a freezer and a van, she was able to buy her own home and furnish it.

These acquisitions meant security and comfort for her family and herself, but they require accumulation of capital. It is difficult for higglers to accumulate capital as most of their money is reinvested in their business. Those who do accumulate capital do so by "throwing partners." This is the informal savings system that is called "throwing box" in Guyana and "susu" in Trinidad. This system works essentially the same way in all three countries. Like Didi, Miss Tiny was able to acquire her house, van and equipment through this savings system. In Jamaica "throwing partners" is a system in which both men and women participate. This informal savings system is found in other areas of the world. It is possible that the system in the Caribbean originated in Africa. Anthropologists have found a similar system, also called susu, among the Yoruba in Nigeria.

In 1980, the van was stolen and her life as a fishwoman came to an abrupt end. She entered into a new phase of higglering. She became an international higgler, one of the hundreds of Caribbean women who travel to Puerto Rico, Panama, the Bahamas, the Cayman Islands and the Virgin Islands to buy and sell. Because of the currency restriction in Jamaica, higglers could not accumulate enough capital to buy the items in these countries. What they did then was enter into a complex system of trade. Items that were scarce or desirable in those countries which were available in Jamaica, were bought and taken over by plane. Miss Tiny's main territory was Panama. On her first trip she went with a friend who was already in the business and who had an intricate system of contacts. The scallion and rum and thyme brought from Jamaica would be sold to these contacts. In this way, the women would acquire the money for the next step: the purchase of items that were both needed and scarce in Jamaica.

> Is we di higglers bring in things that people want and you can't get. We bring in elastic when you couldn't get it and razor blades and all dem kinda things. And now they say how higglers overcharge. Nobody know how hard we work and struggle to bring dem things in. If they don't want we to work this way then they should find something for we to do.

Higglering in Jamaica is an intricate and carefully built system of checks and balances. It is a female system which could not survive on money alone. Almost everything is done on trust. A woman must establish a credible reputation. Produce is sold to one woman who goes to market and then returns with payment. A woman must be careful not to alienate other higglers who buy from her wholesale, because she might lose a steady source of income. Similarly those who buy must always try to pay otherwise they may lose their source of supply and jeopardize their business. In Jamaica, higglers run a business based on respect, fair price and a mutual understanding of the need to survive. It combines business with sisterhood, for no one could make it as a higgler if she did not have the support and trust of other women. In order to survive they must get what they can but never at the price of alienating each other. When Miss Tiny lost her van, it was another woman who helped her to get established in the international trade business. Other women watch your goods when you leave your spot during the day, other women will tell you what the going price is and what is reasonable to ask for. This network is essential to higglering.

In Jamaica the image of a higgler is that of a tough woman who is aggressive and suspicious of outsiders. Higglers, they say, made a lot of money during the economic and political crises in Jamaica. The higglers argue that during the crisis it was they who went out on King Street and sold necessary items, risking theft and violence.

> When all of dem leave de country and taking their money and
> shut up their business, is we higglers who stay right here.
> Some higglers get on bad but is only dem that is new. Most
> higglers who know business will never do that. They can't
> blame all higglers for what some do.

Miss Tiny is now fifty-six years old. She has been a tray girl,
a food shop owner, a fishwoman and now a higgler dealing in
international trade. She has many worries: dealing with customs
officers, paying her bills, holding on to what she has. She worries about the injustice of losing her van and not having any hope
of recovering it. What will happen to higglers and what could
she do if she could not do higglering?

Miss Tiny's hand is slightly maimed. The years in fish and ice
have taken their toll. A few years ago a fish bone pierced her hand
and it became infected. There are other marks on Miss Tiny's life
and body that reflect the struggling times of a higgler. Her eyes
are worn, her voice rasps because it has argued and agitated all
her life and her life is like that of many other women in her
business. She went a little beyond the others by buying a van.
To many, it may not seem like a significant act; to a higgler it
signifies success. She became a model for other higglers to
emulate.

Is a person who makes something out of nothing, who can feed
three children on thirty cents, educate and clothe them just on
her creativity and refusal to fail less heroic than a person who
writes many books, or wins elections, or makes records? Miss
Tiny speaks for herself and for all higglers when she says:

> I should get a medal every Heroes' Day as a one woman. The
> government should give me a medal. Every Heroes' Day I
> should get a gold medal to go through all these troubles and
> nobody don't give me a ting. Is me and me alone. Every
> Heroes' Day I should get a medal, for I struggle hard with my
> life and for my children I is a hero.

Olive Valmont

September 13, 1921
Business Woman
St. Lucia

The Valmont business is St. Lucia's third largest. Run by Olive Valmont and her husband, the business has a wide range of departments — furniture, electrical appliances, lumber, shoes, housewares, cosmetics, haberdashery and so on. Although both husband and wife run this business, they each run separate sections because their business and leadership styles are different.

Olive Valmont was born the thirteenth of September, 1921 in Castries, St. Lucia. Her parents were business people and it is here that she became exposed to business. Olive had a keen interest in what was happening in the shop and became engrossed in it during her summer vacations. Her father died just after she finished high school and although she had brothers and sisters, her mother decided that Olive should be the one to help her run the business. Olive was not quite sure what she wanted to do, but since she loved books, she thought that she might like to further her education.

Her parents' business was medium-sized, with twelve to fifteen employees and Olive ran it with her mother. Soon after Olive married, her husband left his job and joined the business. They opened their own dry goods store in 1951. From that store the Valmont Company grew. At first they had one store on that block; now the whole block and a series of additional stores belong to them. Like her mother she also wanted her children involved in the business; of seven children, two of her daughters are currently very active in it.

The Valmont business, which started as a modest dry goods store, now employs over two hundred people. Olive Valmont has a reputation of being a very tough, exacting woman to work for.

> My husband is quite lenient, I would say, with the staff. Now I am not a tyrant, but I feel that if you have a job to do you ought to get the job done, because that's the only way you could get results. Why settle for half-way measures because half-way measures don't give results.

Running a business requires both toughness and understanding, and after over forty-three years in business Olive Valmont understands these principles intimately. A business cannot be run on personality, whim or indulgence. It is run by hard work, being constantly aware of customer needs and a "nose" for what will sell and what will not.

There is a stereotype that many people do not want to work in the Caribbean. That they simply want to show up and "lime" and sit around chattering, not getting the job done. This is a common complaint of many business people in the region.

> I think that you can motivate people to work. You can try this by keeping all the lines of communication open. To me I would say this is the key to success in a business. Because

> when people feel that they can come to you, you can avoid all
> the problems that set in sometimes and cause all this bad
> feeling. It is important to show people by example. I can never
> be a business person who goes to an office and just give
> people orders and go and sit down. Before I get to work I just
> touch bases even if it's just two minutes with every depart-
> ment. I always make it a point to just pass through.
> Sometimes there is a problem, and some of the girls will say,
> you know, I am in this department and nobody tells me
> anything, but they can't say that about me because I am
> always there.

This constant interaction is for two purposes — to increase her
availability to the staff and to find out the everyday details of the
business — what is selling, what is not, what people are asking
for, what things should be reduced and so on. Even though Olive
Valmont has the reputation of being exacting, she makes sure
that the staff know that she is interested in them.

> People like to feel that you take an interest in them, and that
> is very important. When a person comes in, talk to them. You
> went on vacation, what happened, did you enjoy it? Did you
> do so and so? Just that is enough to make them feel different.
> I think this is important.

A business then requires a great deal of sensitivity towards
people's feelings. However, a successful business is not based only
on sensitivity towards the staff or keeping the lines of communication open. It is also based on reputation. Olive Valmont has a
reputation for being scrupulously honest.

> I don't think you have to be dishonest. The point is that you
> have the intelligence, because you have the ability to make it,
> so why be shady, because you can make it. I know that if you
> have a good name you can make money. I can order a
> thousand pounds or ten thousand pounds of goods. When I
> ask for such an order, they don't question whether I would
> pay. I am always in the accounting department making sure
> that the bills are paid. I say, pay the people their money.
> When once they have that faith in us, then we are O.K.

Running a large company entails a lot of traveling. Buying trips
are necessary, as buying and selling is the core of the company.
Olive Valmont is a successful businesswoman because she has

an aggressive attitude towards buying. She will get on a plane immediately if she knows that there is a commodity worth pursuing.

> It comes almost naturally. The thing is that opportunities are not going to present themselves every day. You know that when you get one you will just have to act on it. The question of traveling: You see all the business people around the Caribbean, I know most of them, and someone would say, 'oh, Mrs. Valmont, there is a show in Trinidad, how about it man, come down for two or three days,' and I am gone. It is just one of the things you have to do.

Olive Valmont developed her keen sense of business because it is the only life she has known. It was what her parents did, it is what she now does, and does well. She knows what will sell and what will not and she at all times conducts her affairs with the highest standards.

> Despite the fact that people will think that I am hard, they would all respect me in the end, because it is better to have their respect than their love. When people respect you, you tell them to do something they do it, they see your side of it, they think you're right, they follow.

The Valmont business is run by a husband and wife team and it is together that they have been able to build the company to what it is today. Many women work in such businesses with their husbands, sometimes the woman gets the credit, sometimes she does not. The woman is very often said to be the strength or the brains behind the business, that it is not really the husband who does all the brilliant things. This societal belief of the man in front and the woman behind is unfair to both men and women. Aggressiveness is not a male perogative and if a woman chooses to be and a man not to be aggressive they should not be considered less a woman or a man.

Ms. Valmont is not the strength *behind* the business, she is a power in the business just as her husband is. She is a simple woman who is always moving and always thinking. Her contribution to the business has been her unscrupulous honesty, her emphasis on communication and people, her business instincts and her demand for respect at all times.

The things you want, you have to work towards them, and sometimes it entails a lot of sacrifice. A person does not get suddenly successful. Success comes only by hard work.

She continues to work not only to make a profit, but because business is a constantly changing field and therefore constantly challenging and also because

It is the only thing I know.

Women in the Church

The church is in very many ways like the women's organizations. Often it is here that women first learn to perform, to take on public responsiblities and to organize. As in politics, women generally make up the bulwark of the organization and yet are excluded from its formal leadership. Many women profiled in other sections could also be included here: Flora Pascal, who cleans the church, decorates and sings in the choir; Millicent Iton, and Ann Liburd. The role of religion in Nisa Ally's, Edna Yorke's and Didi's lives is salient. However, in this section, we have profiled only one woman, Judith Geraldine Weekes.

In the early 80s, Reverend Weekes was one of the few ordained ministers in the region with her own church. This profile provides a good opportunity to look at the role of established and non-established churches regarding the place of women in the church. Why are the institutions of religion whose congregations are heavily female so unclear about the role of women in spiritual leadership of the church? Is it divinely ordained that women cannot be pastors of their own congregations? There are those who argue that it is not and those who argue that it is. The level of discussion has gone on in many churches and is often not resolved.

The following items appeared in *The Nation* in 1987.

> The bishop, the Rt. Reverend Graham Leonard, 65, third-ranking prelate in the state church, called on opponents of women clergy to make an immediate start on planning for an historic split.

> Father Henderson Broome, a prominent West Indian Episcopal priest in Boston, complained that 'remnants' of colonialism in the Caribbean were preventing bishops and the province of the church from moving first to accept women into the priesthood.

Women have dealt with this inadequacy of the church in several ways. One way is steeped in the folklore and culture of the Caribbean. The role of women in Pocamania in Jamaica, Shango practices, voodoo and obeah varies throughout the region. In

Pocomania for example the leader is a high priestess called Queenie.

Judith Geraldine Weekes chose a church that allowed women to be ordained and have their own congregations. Women can conduct marriages, bury the dead and lead their congregations in times of joy and sorrow. It is for women still a non-traditional role in the church and one worth pursuing by other women. Reverend Weekes chose a non-established church to minister in, but there are other women who have chosen to stay in the established churches and fight for a place of authority in it.

Regardless of the church it is the women who attend the services, who ensure that their children go to church, who clean the churches, who bake the cakes to raise money for the church and who see to it that the church is in order. Women should be given the option of pastoring congregations like Reverend Weekes.

Reverend Judith G. Weekes

October 28, 1924
Ordained Minister
Trinidad and Tobago

When Judith Geraldine Weekes was a little girl, her greatest ambition was to get married.

> I wanted to get married and to have four children, three boys and one girl. I wanted to stay home and be a housewife and make jams and jellies.

Her dreams may have had a lot to do with her voracious reading. In her books the heroine often got married, stayed at home and lived happily ever after. Wherever her dream came from, it is not uncommon among dreams of many young women.

Although Judith's life in many ways was different than her mother's there were more similarities than she would have imagined when she was growing up. She, like her mother, raised her children alone, and she, like her mother, worked as a teacher to do this. Both her father and her own husband were absent.

Judith Geraldine Weekes was born on the 28th of October, 1924. There are many outstanding things about her, but perhaps the most outstanding and unusual is that she is an ordained minister. She pastors and administers the Church of the Christ Circle for Better Living. It is unusual for a woman to be an ordained minister of any church. Although the Caribbean has many lay women preachers, their role is very limited. It is rare to see a female minister conducting marriage ceremonies or administering the last rites. However, it is not unusual for women to preach or teach in Sunday schools. Women are rarely on the church boards, the decision-making body of the church. The Caribbean Council of Churches estimates that women make up over seventy percent of all congregations, yet they are not in positions of leadership. They do practically everything else except make policy and pastor. Should a woman choose to become a minister or a board member, she should have the right to pursue and gain these positions.

Until recently many established churches did not allow women to become ordained ministers. In the Caribbean, the Methodist and the Anglican churches have agreed in principle to the ordination of women. However, this is only in principle. At this point Caribbean women, like other women, must face the reality of sexism in the church. Pastoring has been and remains a male-dominated field, and both the church and society blatantly encourage this.

Judith Weekes has taught all her life. She was both a teacher and vice-principal of Diego Martin Junior Secondary School. How does a school teacher who simply wanted to be a mother and housewife end up becoming a reverend? Judith Weekes says that it was not planned, that it was just something that evolved out of the circumstances of her life.

There was a period in her life when she was experiencing pro-
found emotional upheaval. Her marriage was floundering and
for a woman who believed in romance and "happily-ever-after"
this was traumatic. Being a religious woman, she turned to the
church for support and guidance. What she found was a fatalism
to accept her life the way it was which encouraged her to have
a passive belief in God. She rejected orthodox religion but remained unhappy. At that time she discovered the New Thought
Movement. The New Thought Movement appealed to Judith
Weekes because it interpreted Christianity and belief in God in
a radically different way. It argued that every individual had the
right

> to look at things with his (sic) own eyes — to see the Truth as
> it presents itself to him — to interpret that truth by the light
> of his own reason, intuition and spiritual discernment, and to
> let it manifest and express through him in its own manner ...
> Such a man finds within that which he seeks. He does his
> own thinking, and recognizes no man or woman as an
> authorized interpreter of that which can only be interpreted by
> one's own soul ...[1]

This was a spiritual message to take her life and her future into her own hands. She had to think positively, act on her beliefs
and always be cognizant of the truth or the reality of her own
life. Judith Geraldine Weekes plunged into this philosophical
movement so avidly that she is now the president of the International New Thought Movement. This activity led her into many
avenues including the Unity Church and finally the Christ Circle
for Better Living. Her spiritual interest facilitated her travel to the
United States, where she became involved in the Christ Circle
for Better Living and was ordained as a minister of that church
in 1974.

It has been argued that the Church's approach to God and wor-
ship as passive rather than active has been detrimental to women
who represent the majority of the congregation. By encourag-
ing passivity rather than challenge and critical thinking, women
are kept in their place. Certainly Judith Weekes' rejection of the
orthodox church was closely connected to her needs as a woman.
It is interesting that the philosophy she chose encouraged independent thinking and the "Kingship of Self". This is a concept

that is not ingrained in women who were raised to be housewives and mothers. In a way she was rejecting not only the old definition of the church but the old definition of herself. It is not surprising, therefore, that The Church of the Christ Circle for Better Living is headed by a woman and that there are as many women ordained in this church as men. God, love, truth and action are key principles in this church. The head of this denomination feels that:

> Love is that magnificent power called gravity which holds all earthly creatures on this planet. Love is always feminine in character and is the Holy-Mother principle.

This belief in the power of humanity which did not exclude women, armed and guided Judith Geraldine Weekes' life.

Judith Weekes is a soft and gentle woman who lights up when she smiles. She is a loving woman to her congregation and friends. Her ministry is a continuation of her teaching, for she is always a teacher. Touching is a part of her ministry and is something she does with the ease and practice of a woman who has raised four children, taught hundreds of children and held the hands of those she pastors in times of pain and in times of happiness.

Her congregation calls her Judith. She has been a seamstress, bookkeeper, hairdresser, University graduate, wife, mother, teacher and now ordained minister. The members of her congregation all agree that "You always leave her sermons with something." Reverend Weekes describes one of her sermons. She sees her ministry as one which mandates her to teach the importance of self-respect, self-reliance, love and positive and critical thinking. This is a lesson on prayer.

> I wanted to do an exercise. This one on prayer. And so often as soon as you ask people to pray, they start to beg God for this, that and the other. I think that when people can pray as a communication of the spirit, I believe that it would help them much. They would be more reassured that their prayer would be answered. But sometimes people say words but do not pray and so there is no response and I have been saying that for quite a while and I didn't think that they were understanding me at all. I thought they were just listening to me cheerfully, and then I was looking up at the lights and

said to myself, 'you know, this would be a good example. That if I turned off the light, I could pray all I want, the light will not respond until I do something,' because people feel that you pray and it is up to God to do something. So I am in church and in the midst of it I remember that that thought had come and I went to the light and turned it off. I turned around and said, 'Start praying for the light to come back on because there is current.' So they started to pray, saying 'please light, come' and nothing happened and they looked at me waiting, and I said, 'call it, let it come on.' They were not too sure what to do and then they started to say, 'come on light, come on light.' Then I went and turned it on and I said: 'There, it is not for God to do. It is for you to do. It is you who must do something about a situation to change it.'

[1]William Walker Atkinson, *The Law of the New Thought*, page 12.

Women in Health

In the field of health, nurses, nurse/midwives and health aides are positions which are largely held by females. In this section there are three women profiled; Sarah Baptiste, a nurse/midwife, Nita Barrow, a nurse educator and Gweneth Louise O'Reilly, a doctor. Dr. O'Reilly became the first woman to practice medicine at Holberton Hospital and also became its medical superintendent. Administrative positions for women in health are still not common, even though great strides in this area have been made. It is because Dr. O'Reilly returned home to work that she was able to set the precedent for other women.

Nita Barrow, a pioneer Caribbean woman, helped establish the nursing education faculty at the University of the West Indies. This woman, who was convenor of the Decade of Women Non-Governmental Forum in Nairobi, who was on the Eminent Person's group to South Africa, is now Barbados' permanent representative to the United Nations, and may be the next president of the General Assembly of the U.N. Her life has been one devoted to health, women and the Caribbean.

One of the truly "heroic" women in this book is Sarah Baptiste. This Carib woman has served the Carib people for many years and now rolls out cocoa sticks to make a living. Because nurse/midwives had only minimal training, they were not seen as trained nurses even though they did much more than deliver babies. As a result, such women are not entitled to a pension when they retire. Here again is an example of both discrimination against women and elitism. Nation builders like nurse Baptiste should not have to worry about their survival in the last days of their lives.

Yet we have come far; soon seeing a male nurse will not raise eyebrows, it will be accepted as a human service profession. Persons will not be better nurses because they are male or female. One will be judged by one's ability rather than by one's gender.

Sarah Baptiste

November 18, 1902
Pioneer Nurse
St. Vincent and the Grenadines

Sarah Baptiste rode a mule when women rode neither mules nor horses. She rode a bicycle when women did not ride bicycles. She hiked up the steep terrain of the Oweia and Fancy areas, walked to distant villages, and crossed the rough Caribbean waters by canoe to get to the village of Windsor Forest. She did all this to deliver babies and bring health care to the people of these districts. For twenty-five years, she worked in the rural areas in the north of St. Vincent as a nurse/midwife. Since a doctor visited only periodically, nurse Baptiste and the local dispenser were the only resident medical care. Sarah Baptiste is a Carib and lives in the village of Sandy Bay which became a Carib Settlement after the 1946 flood.

The roads leading to Sandy Bay are rough and the village is completely isolated if the Raboca River which crosses the main road is overflowing its banks. There is no electricity, and few shops; everyone must go to the nearest town for necessities. Imagine the isolation and ruggedness of this area when Sarah Baptiste started to practice nursing there twenty-five years ago. The situation was such that she had no choice but to attend to all medical needs of the people. In reality, she did the job of a doctor. She diagnosed illnesses and prescribed cures, delivered hundreds of babies and guided and supported many women during their first childbirth experiences. Over the years they started to call her "mother" for it was she who mothered and cared for the people of Sandy Bay. She was both their spiritual and emotional leader. Sarah Baptiste was a pioneer nurse, but more importantly, she was a pioneer Carib woman.

The striking thing about nurse Baptiste is her lack of self-importance. She does not think of herself as a pioneer, she thinks of herself as "nurse".

> I want people to remember me as Nurse. I want them to say "Oh she was an excellent nurse. She was loving, giving and kind to everyone, to the community, to outside people...'

Nurse Baptiste was born on November 18, 1902, in Camden Park, St. Vincent. At the age of four she was put in the care of Mrs. DaSilva, who was an acquaintance of Sarah's mother and wanted to raise Sarah. The Caribbean family takes a variety of forms. Mrs. DaSilva was in an economically secure family and this was crucial to Sarah's mother.

The Caribs have been poor and at a disadvantage since the Europeans arrived and colonized them. Their skills and culture became suddenly irrelevant when European values were imposed on them. As a result, Carib children were born into a life of poverty. One way to guarantee your children some security was to have them raised by a family in better circumstances. The child was not adopted in the usual sense, and there were some unwritten expectations on the part of the family who raised the child. It was often expected that the child would become a household helper. They were part of the family, but with a very clearly defined role. These girls would be given an elementary education and then lead a life of domestic service.

Over the years Sarah Baptiste's duties evolved as that of nanny. She stayed with the DaSilvas in this capacity until she went to work with a relative of the DaSilvas. Soon she was a young woman and her adopted family decided to arrange her marriage with a young man from Sandy Bay. She was not in love with him but her "family" thought it was an excellent idea, and that it was good for her to be a respectable married lady. Sarah acquiesced, was married and moved to Sandy Bay to live with her husband. There she continued to work as a nanny and a domestic in the estate homes in the area.

At the age of forty she decided to end her marriage. It had been an unhappy experience and she had worked at it for eighteen years. In the end, she felt that she would be happier alone. She had one daughter who by this time had grown up. At that time in 1942, this was an unusual thing for a woman to do. Women who chose to end marriages were frowned upon and they were seen as failures. Women were expected to stay married regardless of their own happiness; they were supposed to make sacrifices for the family and for the marriage. Even if a woman chose to end a marriage it was unlikely for her to do so at the age of forty. This was an age when most people accepted the circumstances of their lives. Sarah Baptiste was not "most people". Ending her marriage at that time was an act of courage.

If Nurse Baptiste had not been employed, it would have been very difficult for her to end her marriage. Many women stayed in unhappy marriages because they were financially dependent. But Sarah had always worked and had always had some financial independence on her small income as a domestic. At the end of her marriage, she was working as a domestic on the Fancy estate. One day the estate owner came into the room where she was washing and said, "Sarah I need a nurse for my estate. How would you like to be a nurse on my estate?" She felt quite surprised and scared, wondering whether she could actually become a nurse, but she said, "Oh yes please Sir, I would be so happy."

The next month she was enrolled in the midwife training programme at Kingstown General Hospital. At forty she was the
oldest trainee. All the others were quite young. The only people
her age were the trainers.

> Oh I was very embarrassed. Because I was a Carib and a
> domestic, some of the girls would speak to me very cross.
> I was vexed but I smiled. They sent me to clean out the
> sewage and I have to do it, that was my job, I could not have
> frowned too much but I smiled. Still in my heart I was vexed
> and did many different things that they told me to do that
> they did not want to do themselves, but I did it because I
> wanted to become a nurse.

After her training she returned to the village of Sandy Bay where
she practiced for twenty-five years. The life of a nurse in her
district was hard and demanding. If she had had children and
a husband, it would have been very difficult to do it. People came
to her house at all times. One morning at two a.m. an expecting
father came for her to help his wife in her delivery. He came from
Windsor Forest and she was stationed for that week in Fancy,
another remote village, accessible only by canoe. Nurse Baptiste
got herself ready, jumped in the father's canoe and paddled with
him to the woman's house. The baby was delivered with Nurse
Baptiste present. She went whenever she was called and by
whatever means she could. In the twenty-five years that she has
helped women in delivery no one died in childbirth. She says,

> No one, no one in all the years I have been delivering up to
> now, no one has ever died in childbirth, thanks to God.

People in a small village need more than medical care. The
church, the Girl Guides, The Mother's Union were organizations
that she spearheaded. The Minister came every Sunday to conduct service but because of the inaccessibility of the village, he
was often unable to come. It was Mother who conducted the service. It was Mother who started Sunday School in the village. It
was Mother who started the Girl Guides and the Mother's Union.
    One measure of a people's trust and esteem is to look at those
they turn to in moments of crisis. When Mrs. Gordon's eighteen-
year-old daughter died she called in her pain and grief "Send
for Mother". Joan Cambridge set her wedding date for June 10th.

The first person she went to was Nurse Baptiste. "Mother," she said, "I want to get married on June 10th. Can you help us? You know what to do." Everyone relies on Nurse Baptiste, for there is no question in their minds that she knows what to do. "You know many a times I don't know what I am going to do or say but I have to be there."

Nurse recalls one incident. One day a woman's husband was about to beat her and in the uproar the woman shouted, "Oh God Mother help me." Nurse ran quickly to the house and banged on the door.

"Carl," she said, "open this door, this is Mother. I said open this door."

Carl opened the window which was just above the stairway. He shouted, "Mother, stay out of this, stay out of this, Mother."

Nurse wasted no time, she jumped through the window and held on to Carl's hand. He had a stick in his hand and was hostile. She continued to hold onto his hand.

"Carl," she said in a commanding voice, "peace be still, I say peace, be still, the Lord said to the rough seas, peace be still. Peace be still Carl!"

He paused, and was able to control himself.

Sarah Baptiste has fought a life-long battle against the injustices wrought on women and she had tried to teach women self-respect and self-protection. She continues to live in Sandy Bay, a small village by the sea. She is now retired and makes cocoa sticks to earn some money. As she sits at her kitchen table rolling them out, women, children, men come over to talk, to joke and to buy a few sticks.

"Morning Mother how you today!"

"Old Nurse not too bad today darlin, but look at dis child nose running. Come take this kerchief and wipe your nose."

The sea practically rushes up her kitchen window where she sits, a remarkable woman who jumped through a window at the age of 79 to still Carl's hand. A pioneer of the village of Sandy Bay, a leader by any standard, and she sits rolling out cocoa sticks on her kitchen table. This Carib woman who loves her people and whose life has been filled with unconscious acts of courage, is a pioneer.

I love the Carib, I love to be amongst the Carib. I am Carib and I am proud.

Ruth Nita Barrow

November 15, 1916
Nursing Educator
Barbados

Nita Barrow has been described as a citizen of the world, but she is in reality a Bajan woman who is part Jamaican, part Guyanese, part Trinidadian, part Antiguan and part Virgin Islander. Although she has lived and worked in the territories mentioned, there is no part of the Caribbean that she has not seen.

She was born in Barbados at Nesfield, St. Lucy, on November 15, 1916. Her younger sister, Ena, was the Associate Director of Public Health in St. Croix; her brother, Errol, was the first Prime

Minister of Barbados and her younger sister, Sybil, was one of the few female pharmacists in the region.

> We are five of us, we were born in three different islands. We knew we were Barbadian and proud of it, there was never any doubt about it, but never considered that we couldn't live anywhere else but Barbados. I have always been proud to be a West Indian. I never felt apologetic anywhere in the world for being a West Indian. I believe if you set out to do a job you must finish it. You don't have to be the best person in your job, but you have to do the best you can in the job, that is the important thing. You have to measure yourself against yourself. Don't always be looking at the other person. There needs to be a great sense of pride developed that the Caribbean is an important part of the world, size does not matter.

Ruth Nita Barrow made her contributions in several arenas; her most prominent contributions were in nursing education and with the YWCA. She worked on the professionalization of nurses and the establishment of quality nursing education. Her accomplishments in all the areas in which she chose to work is phenomenal. One has only to look at a few of the highlights of her career. She was the first World Health Organization Nurse from the Caribbean, the first president of the Jamaica Nurses Association, the first black Caribbean woman to be appointed to a senior post by the Colonial Office in the Caribbean and the first black president of the World Wide YWCA in 1975. Before her retirement in 1980, she was the first woman Director of the Christian Medical Commission (CMC) which is the health arm of the World Council of Churches. She was the convenor of the 1985 NGO forum held in Nairobi, Kenya, and Barbados' prominent representative to the United Nations and the only woman on the eminent person's group which the commonwealth Secretariat appointed to attempt a rapprochement in South Africa.

At the time she was growing up in the 1920s and '30s, women could aspire either to marriage, teaching or nursing.

> There were so few opportunities for girls. It was nursing or teaching. In our family we were not growing up to do nothing, not even if you were getting married. You were expected to be trained in something. I remember somebody asking my grandmother 'why do you educate your daughters? They will all get

married in the end' and she said 'Because when they have children they will also educate them.

Nita chose the nursing field because three of her friends were going into it. The early days of the nursing profession in Barbados at the old General Hospital were difficult.

> It was tough and then you worked terribly hard. We were on twelve hour duty, you got off one evening early. You were on duty from quarter to six in the morning till eight o'clock at night. You got off two hours in the day. If I was off at eight and we had only eight to nine off, my clothes were on in ten minutes and in ten minutes I was gone. We got sixteen shillings and sixteen cents (approximately $4.16) per month and don't forget every thermometer you broke was deducted, and a bed pan was eighteen shillings. One month one of our colleagues broke a bed pan, and she is a very prominent person today. We all went down to sign for our money and we would say to each other 'How much you got this month?' Some would say five shillings, some would say ten shillings and, this day we asked her 'Tell me you much you got?' She said 'My dear I drew my breath.'

The opportunities for training were taken up as they came and Nita Barrow moved from nurse to nursing instructor at the School of Public Health in Jamaica, to consultant for the World Health Organization. For relaxation she became involved in the YWCA. Her activities in the 'Y' and in nursing were always marked by her outspokenness. The people in her family were agitators; her father and her uncle were two of the most notable ones. Her uncle, Charles Duncan O'Neal, led the Barbados Workers Union.

> My father, the tales of him when he went to St. Croix. He was a priest in the Anglican Church and ended up organizing workers out there and founding the African Methodist Episcopal Church in St. Croix. The people worked for twenty-five cents a day, and the Americans were running the place and my father and my sister Sybil's godfather, Hamilton Jackson, organized them into cooperatives. It was reported that during this protest, everybody went down one day to see what was going to happen to the Reverend Barrow who had wrapped himself in the American flag and said 'Touch me if you dare.'

But perhaps the most important influence on her values was her grandmother.

> My grandmother was very much a rebel herself. She had her
> own ideas. We didn't know it at the time, we just absorbed
> them. My grandmother raised us and she was quite an in-
> domitable figure and she told us what to do — a very strong
> person. She was very strict, no boyfriends could stay after ten
> o'clock. She had a routine, she sat on the verandah and spent
> afternoons chatting with everybody passing. We had to do
> lessons during the week. When it came to weekends, there
> was a little more latitude, but at nine o'clock visitors were sup-
> posed to leave. Her bedroom was upstairs. She had a stick
> and at 9:30 p.m. she would quietly pound on the floor. It was
> well known, and I would retreat to the steps to talk. There
> were always standards which had to be observed.

Having been brought up in a family in which her grandmother
ensured high standards and her relatives were agitators, Nita
herself could not fail to be a highly principled outspoken person. But it was not until she joined the YWCA in Jamaica that
her leadership qualities came to the fore. Her first experience
in Jamaica was in the 1940s and '50s.

> I think that I was lucky because of the years I was in Jamaica.
> When I went to Jamaica there was no doubt that the average
> Jamaican woman's involvement in politics and positions of
> responsibility was greater than it was in other territories, and
> that was in the '40s. The average Jamaican woman spoke up
> for herself. I'm not saying they didn't suffer from all the
> disabilities of discrimination but there were examples that a
> woman could reach the top. In the second year when I was
> there, one of the first woman Permanent Secretary was ap-
> pointed. That's a long time ago. Now I don't say that there
> hasn't been one or two since, but that was something positive.
> There were women like Sybil Francis, a Staff Tutor in Social
> Work at UWI; Winnie Hewitt, Winnie Mills, Confidential
> Secretary to the Colonial Secretary; Carmen Lusan, 1st Carib-
> bean Area Secretary of the YWCA and many more. Now these
> were women in the YWCA in Jamaica. In the beginning, to
> qualify for full membership in the YWCA in Jamaica, you had
> to have Senior Cambridge. Nowhere else in the world have I
> ever found that clause. Ms. Heath, the English General
> Secretary who established this requirement in the 'Y', then

combed the Secondary Schools and ensured that the group in this way received what we now call 'leadership training'. When I got there it was democratized. But of course there were many other participants and members who developed their potential in the 'Y' and held responsible posts afterwards.

Although the YWCA in Jamaica was ahead of its time it was once again an example of a women's organization providing the training and professionalism that women needed to become the leaders in their fields.

I lived in the 'Y' hostel. Every evening it was straight from work to the 'Y'. If we were not in Rangers we were doing skills training. If we were not doing skills training we were in a debating society, if not debating we were in a public affairs group. I can thank the 'Y' for any experiences which developed my leadership. They sent me to Beirut to the World YWCA Council Meeting whilst I was a student at Edinburgh University. I was a member of the Board. I was only in the hostel for eight months but continued my interest in the 'Y'. I complained about the hostel committee; they put me on the hostel committee. When I complained about something else they put me on another committee and the next thing I found myself on the Board. We had a very good group in Jamaica. They would be calling them feminists now because when they wouldn't pass the Nurses' bill in Jamaica in 1951, the nurses dressed in their uniforms, the matrons in their falls, and went to the House of Assembly and sat up in the gallery because we heard they were going to debate the Nurses' bill. There was prolonged discussion of a rather negative nature. Bustamante wrote a note, he was leader then, to Sangster who was chairman of his party and leading the debate. He said 'Donald, don't play the fool, you see those women sitting in the gallery, they mean business.

The nursing bill was passed.

In her youth, she was not always achieving and doing remarkable things. When she went to Beirut, she skipped out as often as she could to see the country. At the same meeting, she stood up and invited the delegates to bring the next meeting to Jamaica, having no idea how they would be accommodated or that England had already invited the delegates since they were celebrating 100 years of the 'Y' in their country. This was what the 'Y' provided her with, a chance to make mistakes and to learn from them. Quite outside of the 'Y' exposure, Nita had always displayed a forthrightness and a particular intolerance of injustice.

> I remember when I was a young nurse in Barbados and there were a lot of breakages of dishes and so on in the nurses' hostel. When we went to collect our money at the end of the month everybody had to pay two shillings and sixpence for a plate and in those days a plate was six pence. So I retired to the nurses' hostel, took up a plate, went out on the steps, took a stone, broke it in four and when the Warden complained, I said that was the plate I paid for.

Recently, teachers and nurses have begun to organize and demand better salaries and working conditions. This has taken many by surprise; historically the professions which have been dominated by women — nursing and teaching — were not known for their militancy or union activities. In 1949, Nita Barrow was one of the women who helped to organize nurses in Jamaica.

This background aptly prepared Nita Barrow for her very important work in recent years. She was acclaimed all over the world for her skill, graciousness and talent in convening the Decade of Women non-governmental forum in Nairobi in 1985. There were over 1,300 workshops and thousands of women from the world over. Many of these women were on opposite sides of the political fence and Nita Barrow and her staff ensured the smooth running of this potentially volatile event. In 1986, she was appointed Barbados' permanent representative to the United Nations.

She was in the Commonwealth's eminent person's group which tried to get the opposing parties in South Africa to a negotiating table. In South Africa, a small white South African minority has been in control of the country and has used their power to oppress and deny essential human rights to all persons of colour in that country, particularly the black majority. There has been a great struggle against this white minority both in and outside of South Africa and many have died for this cause in that country.

After meeting all the significant leaders of the struggle in South Africa, Nita left with a feeling of hope rather than despair. She met Nelson Mandela, the great leader of South Africa who has been in prison for over 24 years because of his opposition to the government. "When you meet him you feel like you are talking to a special man and he entertains you as though he is in his home and not in prison — how can you get depressed?" Alan Boesak, a religious leader of the struggle, "spent most of the day being harassed by the police and at 9:30 preached to a church of white, black, coloureds, and indians (they are not allowed to assemble in the same place), the most political sermon, and I said, 'Alan they are going to bring your corpse in,' and he said, 'Don't worry, they are not that foolish.' How can you get less than hopeful?"

She met Desmond Tutu, another religious leader of the struggle.

> One day when he was in Canada he attended the legislature, went to a seminar, walked in an anti-apartheid march, addressed a rally, then went to a football match and arrived at a Harry Belafonte concert that night at 10 p.m. When he went on stage the crowd cheered, and he said — 'what happened to the walls of Jericho when the trumpets blew?' — 'they came tumbling down', the crowd shouted. 'Well that is what is going to happen in South Africa,' Desmond says, and then sashays off the stage with a Michael Jackson step, that brought the house down.

She has received two honorary doctorates, one from MacMaster University in Canada and one from the University of the West Indies, an Honorary Fellow from Royal College of Nursing, Great Britain, and is often addressed by her title Dame Nita. Most people call her Nita. Yet with all the awards and prominence, Ruth Nita Barrow remains a warm and simple person whose lack of pretentiousness is striking.

> I believe that when you accept an award you are only a symbol. It is a symbol of all the people who helped you. It is theirs, it is not yours and therefore you can't give yourself airs on the people.

Nita Barrow never married,

> but that doesn't mean that I haven't had fun or boyfriends. I have enjoyed my life and have never regretted not being married. I have been too busy.

Her generous spirit is marked by principle and very high standards and it is this combination that makes her at once very human and very special. There is a quality about Nita Barrow that makes most people with whom she comes in contact feel valued. In the evenings when she can be quiet she sits in her house in Barbados and watches the sea as the light changes from dusk to night.

Gweneth O'Reilly

October 10, 1923
Medical Doctor
Antigua

G weneth Louise O'Reilly was born in St. John's, Antigua on the 10th of October, 1923. Her father was in business and her mother studied to be a teacher and also worked as a secretary before marrying and raising a family. Gweneth was the third of four children and attended first the T.O.R. Memorial High School and from the age of twelve, the Antigua Girl's High School. She won the Leeward Islands Scholarship in 1941.

The Leeward Islands Colony in the 1940's comprised Antigua-Barbuda, St. Kitts-Nevis-Anguilla, Montserrat, and the British Virgin Islands. A scholarship was awarded yearly on the results of the Cambridge School Certificate examination taken in all the Leewards. Since the Second World War was raging at that time she was not able to leave Antigua before September 1944 and actually did not start her training before 1945. After winning this scholarship, she studied medicine at the Queen's University of Belfast, Northern Ireland. The decision to become a doctor came only after she won the scholarship.

> Otherwise it would not have been possible to do a thing like that at the time.

As late as the 1950s, Dr. O'Reilly was only the second Antiguan woman to become a doctor. The first female Antiguan doctor was Caroline Brown, who qualified in 1938 and practised only for a short time in Antigua before going to Trinidad. There, she married and practiced for a number of years, and subsequently moved to Jamaica.

Although medicine has been a male-dominated field, there have been female physicians throughout history. "One of the medical students to enroll at the male-only Edinburgh College in 1809 was a James Barry who qualified in 1812 to become Dr. James Barry — a name which maintained and shielded the actual and mysterious Miranda Stuart until after her death." (Joan Macksey and Kenneth Macksey, The Book of Women's Achievements, Stein and Day: New York, 1976, p.145).

The document attached to this profile illustrated that Dr. Effield Roden, the first woman to practise medicine in Antigua had great difficulty finding a position as a doctor because she was a woman. She was appointed as a district doctor after her mother wrote the attached letter to the Colonial Office in London.

It was not until the 1930s, about twenty years later, that the first Antiguan woman — Caroline Brown took a course in medicine. Then it was in the 1940's that another Antiguan woman — Gweneth O'Reilly — was able to take up medicine having won the Leeward Island Scholarship, which was available to assist persons belonging to the Leeward Islands Colony to obtain higher education. The other women who won the Leeward Islands

Scholarship after Dr. O'Reilly and became medical doctors were Dr. Lenore Harney (St. Kitts) who became the Chief Medical Officer in Barbados and Dr. Margaret O'Garra (Monserrat) who has been Paediatrician at Holberton Hospital in Antigua.

After completing her medical studies abroad in 1953, Gweneth Louise O'Reilly returned to Antigua where she practised for over twenty years. Antigua, an island of approximately 75,000, has had few female doctors.

> I needed to come back, my only chance of getting a career was from funds donated by the Leeward Islands Government. I was expected to return and I felt that it was right for me to return.

Her return to Antigua was to have historic significance. She was appointed as the first medical officer to reside at Holberton Hospital. Holberton was the only General Hospital in Antigua. Before Dr. O'Reilly, medical care was under the direct supervision of the Surgeon Specialist who was also the Medical Superintendent. There was no doctor resident at the hospital; the Matron would be called first in an emergency and in her absence the Assistant Matron. Dr. O'Reilly's presence made the Matron's task easier during emergencies.

Because there were not as many doctors at the hospital as there are today, Dr. O'Reilly practiced in almost every field of medicine. She assisted in surgery and served as anaesthetist for a period. At varying times, she was in charge of obstetrics, pediatrics and internal medicine.

> Each, in its way, was challenging, but one of the advantages of working in obstetrics was that the majority of patients went home well.

Seeing a patient return home well was what she had been trained to accomplish. It always gave her feeling of satisfaction.

> You do your best for the person. It was all very rewarding particularly when you thought a patient would die and he or she would get well and be able to walk out of hospital.

She retired from Holberton Hospital in 1976 for health reasons, and set up a private part-time practice, working Monday through

Saturday in the mornings. The rest of her time she has for herself.

> Just to do whatever I feel like. I do all sorts of things around
> the house. If I feel like making some jam or jelly I just do it.

During her tenure as resident (until 1963) and up until 1967, there
was no casualty department at Holberton. A major change oc-
curred that year (1967) with the recruitment of three junior
hospital doctos and the opening of casualty. As time passed there
were further additions to the staff thus making it possible to
upgrade the services offered. Her longstanding residency as
Medical Officer at Holberton was a responsibility that required
dedication to duty and a tremendous amount of work.

Antigua is home for Gweneth O'Reilly. It is where her friends
and family are. She chose not to get married and has no children.

> You will find that many of the older professional women did
> not get married. But you won't find that today. It is a little dif-
> ferent now for women. In my time when one was a student
> on a scholarship one couldn't get married. Under the terms of
> some scholarships, for example, the Leeward Islands scholar-
> ship, it was clearly stipulated that should the holder marry,
> the scholarship would cease. In other words one understood
> that it was best to complete the course of study first. Then
> having made the decision one abided by it. Persons differ.
> Some can only manage to cope with one thing at a time, and
> having recognised this fact are content to do whatever is im-
> mediately at hand to the best of their ability. Also if one is the
> only person at a place one must have a sense of responsibility
> and realize that that responsibility comes first. I decided not
> to bother with marriage and I'm not upset in the slightest, not
> in the slightest.

In practicing medicine, Dr. O'Reilly has seen many important
changes in the field.

> There have been many changes, lots of changes. A change in
> equipment and drugs and because of the fast pace of life —
> more violence, more accidents, and consequently, more varied
> and often severe injuries. The treatment for high blood
> pressure has changed. There are now drugs that can be used
> to keep it under control. The older person with diabetes can
> now be treated with tablets taken orally. Smallpox has been

eradicated from the world. Here, immunisation has been established on a regular basis. Now we have blood transfusion as a routine procedure. Before, such a thing was very rare indeed.

Dr. O'Reilly feels that:

> Dedication towards one's job is important. People should try to be honest in whatever they do. Medicine is an interesting career. There are so many areas in it that our young people can find some area in which they can make a contribution. Responsibility is important in all careers and it is always useful to think of the other person's point of view.

She was the first woman to practice medicine full time at Holberton Hospital, the first resident Medical Officer, the second woman to win the Leeward Islands Scholarship, the second Antiguan woman to become a doctor and the one who returned to Antigua to work. She has been President of the Antiguan Planned Parenthood Association and Chairman of the Nursing Council of Antigua. And yet she says modestly:

> My life could have been more useful — I'm sure it could have been more useful. You know that you can't do everything. You just do what you are able to do.

The Public Record Office, London
January 19,1916

                                                  The Bobonne
                                           38 Semster Square
                                                Bayswater W.

Mister Chamberlain Esq.
Mister Saw Esq.

Sirs,

I shall be grateful to you if you will kindly allow me to interest you in the position of my daughter Dr. Effield Roden, M.D. living in Antigua West Indies. I want to ask that she may be given a government post as doctor in that island. She was one of the very first women medical students in England 20 years ago — but at that time there was so much opposition to women doctors that she could get no work in England so she answered an advertisement for an assistant doctor in Antigua West Indies and went there.

She married a sugar planter there. His income is less than £200 a year and she has gathered together a few patients and whenever there has been a vacancy for a doctor she has applied for it but it has always been given to a man. At the present time 2 vacancies have been filled with Americans — which is not fair.

At the present time she is acting as locum tenere for Dr. Cooke of Cedar Hill Antigua, B.W.I. — while he is in England. Owing to the shortage of doctors here he may be thankful to remain if he were offered a post and then my daughter could have his work with his pay out there.

She is a very capable clever woman of over 40 years now and when she arrived in Antigua first she was the only M.D. there — not one of the doctors had obtained that degree. It is only fair that we should have a little recognition for what our children have done.

My son F.A. Greene is a very able engineer and he has given the whole of his time excepting Saturdays for secret government service since the war began. I beg you gentlement to take some interest in this matter. I enclose you my daughter's latest letter that you may see that she is an educated woman and most worthy of the post she solicits.

                                                  gentlemen
                                                  I remain
                                            Yours faithfully
                                           (Mrs.) F. Greene

Women in Organizations

There exists an attitude about traditional women's organizations like the Women's League, and Women's Social Welfare Associations: that women in these organizations do trivial things like bake tarts and cakes and have tea parties. All of this to help their "little causes" and get some "pin" money either for their organizations or for the church or some other good cause. Men's organizations like the Lions or the Rotarians or cricket or football clubs, however, do not suffer from such trivializing: their fundraising is not for "little causes" — it is to "help build the country."

When women organized to address the injustices in women's lives, they were seen as a threat to the family and society. Instead of having bazaars for charity, women were now asking for equal rights. But women who fight for women's rights can be as traditional as Nisa Ally or as non-traditional as Calypso Rose. Women's organizations in and of themselves move women away from the prescribed traditional roles, providing them with far more skills and opportunities.

The contributions made in the traditional women's organizations in this region have been outstanding, and the women in these organizations did advocate for women. It was such organizations that supported the poor, the handicapped, children with limited opportunities and women struggling to raise families alone. The three women in this section are only a very small example of a very large contribution. The invisible nature of such women's work is aptly demonstrated in Nisa Ally's life. Certainly one can argue that Ann Liburd was a feminist. Millicent Iton's life exemplifies the role of women in professional organizaations run predominantly by women. There have been in this region countless such organizations in the form of convent schools, nurseries and kindergartens run by women who have left their mark on their students, the educational system, and on their countries.

The work of organizations like the Caribbean Women's Associations and the Muslim Women's Organization was not required work and there is no way to measure the importance of these contributions to our societies. This building of institutions and society was done by our mothers, grandmothers and great grand-mothers. Their work, whether in the home or in organizations, was done with a deep love for country and family, and it was never at any time trivial or superficial work.

Nisa Ally

May 31, 1927
President, Muslim Women's Organization
Guyana

N isa Ally's whole life was spent raising ten children and helping her husband's business whenever she could. She had
little time for anything else, but she joined the Muslim Women's
Organization and would attend functions and contribute and participate as much as she could. Over the years, she was seen as
a reliable and concerned worker and when the time came to find
a new president, she was elected. She knew that some of the
women in the organization were thinking about her in this capaci-

ty and the idea terrified her. She could not conceive of herself as the president of anything. She would not know what to do, what to say, how to lead, she was convinced that she could not do it.

The day of the election she stayed home. When the women saw that she was not there two of them went to her house to collect her.

> I can't go because I have to look after the children. I have to stay with them.
>
> I will stay with them. You go ahead, I will look after them for you. You don't have to worry, I have three children myself, we come to take you, Mrs. Ally, and you have to go.
>
> But I am not tidy, I can't go so.
>
> You look clean to me, nothing wrong with you. Go along, people there waiting on you. Look, Mrs. Bacchus will take you.

She sat through the nomination process wondering what she could do, feel nervous and embarrassed. After the elections were over she had to say something. Shyly she got up and said:

> I thank you for the honor, but you will have to help me because I have a lot to learn.

She sat down feeling a great sense of panic and many of the women came up to her as she sat and told her that they would help and that she should just call them if she wanted anything done. This support calmed her and she felt that with the support of women maybe it wouldn't not be so bad.

Her life has been directed by two things - her family and her religion — Islam. She was born on the 31st day of May, 1927 in Skeldon, Guyana. Approximately half of the population of Guyana is of East Indian descent. A substantial number of this population is Muslim. Although there are Muslims of African descent in Guyana, the overwhelming majority are Indo-Guyanese. Three of the world's major religions are practised by substantial numbers of the Guyanese population - Christianity, Hinduism and Islam. There are Muslim and Hindu women's organizations as there are Christian ones. The organization of which Nisa Ally became president is the Rafaat ki Jamaat - the Organization of Muslim Women, She has been President of this organization since 1965. It is not that she has been unwilling to relinquish the presidency - it is just that few women wanted to take on the job. In Ms. Ally's case, the presidency was literally thrust upon her.

> I've been doing it so long because nobody want to take the job. They are afraid people will criticise them if they make a decision, that somebody won't like it. You have to learn that sometimes you have to stop trying to please everybody all the time. When you're in a role like mine people will criticize you no matter what you do.

When she took over the Rafaat ki Jamaat the treasury contained the princely sum of twenty dollars. Her immediate goal was to make the organization independent.

> I wanted to see that the organization is independent in the way of assets and cash.

Under Nisa Ally's leadership the women organized bazaars and film shows to raise money. This is an activity that is typical of many women's organizations, but it is an activity that has funded many other organizations and charities. For the Rafaat ki Jamaat this activity provided assets and a way to generate an ongoing income. From twenty dollars they grew to become the owners of cooking and eating utensils for large gatherings, over two hundred chairs and a public address system. This equipment was hired out on a regular basis to other organizations or functions like weddings and brought a regular income for the organization. There are about four hundred women who belong to this organization. For the Muslim families who are poor, the organization offers free burial, small grants for those whose children might be in legal trouble, support in cases of fire and other disasters, and wheelchair or other aids to the disabled. All of these services are integrated with the observance of Islamic holy days and are in keeping with the principles of Islam.

The presidency of the Rafaat ki Jamaat taught Nisa Ally self-confidence and toughness. There were many difficult moments. She did not mind criticisms in general, but when the criticism became personal she felt hurt. The criticism ranged from her appearance after she became president to using the organization's money for her own purposes. These were all petty and concocted stories. One rumour in particular caused her much grief, but the committee in the organization refused to accept her resignation.

For a person whose experience was of her own family, this was a rude awakening to a world outside of those who loved her. The process gave her strength and confidence and an ease in conducting herself in public.

> I find that I can more face people now and I can meet people. I'm not shy and I think I'm more fluent. I could converse - and now I can talk without making notes and so, now I find if I make notes, it keeps me back. If I have to say something I prefer to just say it. Now if I go to a function I don't have to be asked. If I feel something has to be said I just say it.

This growth is one of the singular advantages for women in women's organizations. This change in self-confidence has been striking for many women; Ann Liburd, Reverend Judith Weekes and Nisa Ally all demonstrate this.

If the job of the president of an organization was a paid position which was being advertised as vacant, Nisa Ally would never have dreamed of applying for it. No one would conceive of hiring her either. After all, what experience did she have? She spent all of her time at home and as a part-time accountant in her husband's business.

The nature and context of women's organizations made this possible for Nisa. On the surface, it would seem that she had no training for a leadership position, but this would be a very narrow view of her life experience. A woman who has had ten children: six girls and four boys, all of whom are successful people with their own careers, is not to be easily discounted. Raising and educating ten children requires not only leadership skills, but stamina and determination. All of her six daughters have careers of their own. Two of them are language teachers, one is a mathematics teacher, one is completing her Ph.D., and two are accountants. She has a son that is a lecturer at the University of Guyana, two in business for themselves and one who resides in Canada. She had three basic objectives for her children:

> I wanted them all to have an education. I wanted them to know Islam and I wanted them to be independent and have their own careers and not be dependent on the family business.

A careful look at her objectives for the Rafaat ki Jamaat will show that they are almost the same as those for her ten children. Financial independence, skills development, religious observance and perseverance.

Education is of critical importance to Nisa Ally and it was with an attitude of learning that she approached her task. The concern with education stemmed from her childhood. Her mother had wanted Nisa to go as far as she could in school. Nisa herself had wanted to go on to secondary school and become a teacher, but she was not allowed to do so. At that time it was felt that girls fourteen and fifteen years old should be married rather than at school. With such priorities, further education for a girl would be pointless. Nisa Ally's completion of primary school was an act of defiance by her own mother who was only allowed to attend primary school for three years. After the three years she stayed at home and was initiated into housework. This was not what Nisa Ally's mother wanted for herself, she wanted to go further and she vowed that her daughter would have more education. She did, but it was still not enough for Nisa who in turn vowed that her children would have as much education as they wanted. It took two generations of strong willed women to achieve this educational freedom.

> My brother said that the girls take after me, I don't know. I always wanted to be a teacher and I always pushed them and my mother had wanted me to go more but her parents didn't want me to so I pushed my children. Yes, I pushed them.

The Muslim and Hindu communities were at first leery of the school system. Their biggest fear was that the school system would convert their children away from Islam and Hinduism. They felt that their daughters should be married and they needed the labour in the sugar and rice fields. This fear of cultural erosion was deeper at the time Nisa's mother was in school, but it slowly abated over time. Education has been seen by many Caribbean people as a way out of poverty. For Nisa Ally, education was the way out for her daughters. She wanted them to have an education of their own and to be economically independent. It was a stepping stone to freedom.

Nisa Ally was married at the age of sixteen, her marriage was arranged and her husband, who is a butcher, is also very active in the Muslim community. It is because of her dedication to Islam that she became involved in the Muslim Women's organization. The work of the organization is essential to poor members of the Muslim community. Many women who have raised children and have not worked outside their home, involve themselves in such organizations. The work and activities of these organizations are never, on a national scale, seen as significant contributions to the society at large. Perhaps the most important reason for this under-valuing is that neither the work of a housewife or volunteer is paid work. Yet the essential services that these women provide are particularly crucial to countries that cannot afford the large expenditure that would ensure that the poor do not go hungry, homeless and unclothed. It is women's organizations that fulfill these needs.

It is the duty of every Muslim who can afford it to make a pilgrimage (also called Haj) to Mecca where the Prophet Muhammed lived and practised Islam. It is Nisa Ally's dream to do this. She wants to go but that means leaving the organization for a substantial period of time. This absence will create the space for a new leadership.

> The ladies have to decide what they want. I will go to Haj and I want to go and see my son in Canada and make a little trip. I feel it is time for me to take a little time off.

The role of a mother, particularly in a large family, often requires that person to put the needs of others before her own needs. Many women, after years of raising a family, become so accustomed to putting off their own needs that they find it difficult to put themselves first. The habit of serving others is hard to break, and Nisa Ally, after all these years, has decided that she will do something for herself - take some time off. The self-confidence that she gained in running the affairs of the organization affected other areas of her life as well. She can now use that same self-confidence for herself.

Nisa Ally is a devout Muslim woman.

> I believe that religion is important and character is important. I feel that we must have a responsibility to the community -

that people must not look down on you, they must look up to you. This is in any society whether it is Muslim or not.

There are those who think that Muslim women are supposed to be followers rather than leaders, that they are supposed to stay at home and have children and that they are supposed to be docile and reticent. No one can question Nisa Ally's status as a Muslim. Yet she is not docile, she is a leader. She is vocal, and an example in her community of motherhood and leadership. This is her way of being a good citizen. It took two generations of women in her family (her mother and herself) to have the right to be fully educated. Her life is an example that being a good Muslim is the same as being a good citizen, a good mother and an effective leader.

Millicent Iton

April 3, 1928
Director, CANSAVE
St. Vincent and the Grenadines

CANSAVE is an organization that focuses on human development. It starts with the welfare and education of children and then extends to the teaching of parenting skills and the training of kindergarten teachers.

> If you are going to be a developmental organization to touch people's lives and help them to self-reliance then you can't confine yourself to just caring for the children. A child is just one entity in the family and if you are going to help the fami-

ly, then I think you have to get a deeper involvement with other family members rather than just the child. Some families might need help with nutrition, some might need help with education and sometimes the mother needs employment, so we try to be responsive to these various needs.

CANSAVE was started by the English before it was taken over by the Canadians. It was known as the Save The Children's Fund and its objective was to provide nutrition and education to children of nursery school age. These objectives have since evolved and expanded into an organization concerned with early child development and family life. Millicent Iton is the president of CANSAVE in St. Vincent. She was born in Georgetown, St. Vincent on the third of April 1928. She has been married for over thirty-two years and has four sons. The person who influenced her life when she was a child in Georgetown was her grandmother.

My grandmother was a very dynamic woman and I remember so much about her. She always used to say, 'whatever you do always aim for perfection.' She was a great reader and a great talker and she used to say, 'never be afraid, once you have truth and you have conviction, never be afraid because the truth will set you free.' She also liked public speaking. I remember when representation had to be made for the village she would address the governor and such persons. There was always something so upstanding about her; I admired her. She would say, you have a voice, you got to have character and you must hold yourself upright, a woman should always be upright and these are some of the things that remain with me.

The profile of CANSAVE in St. Vincent is that of a highly professional organization that provides quality education and social services. Millicent Iton started in CANSAVE in 1966 and became its president in 1972. Before her involvement with CANSAVE she worked as a primary school teacher, was a civil servant for a short while and then stayed home and raised her four sons.

Before we were married we agreed on this, that I would stay at home and raise the children. When we had achieved that and they had reached a certain age, by that time I was quite tired of the house. When they had gone to school time was heavy on my hands. I discussed this with my husband and I decided to go out to work and I went out and made it work.

After she decided to embark on a career, she had to take up training opportunities abroad. This she did with her husband's support and encouragement. It was envisioned that she take charge of the operations as the British and then the Canadians phased themselves out. In the Caribbean, with the advent of independence and the departure of the British, many people felt that the local people could not run the organizations as efficiently and professionally as the English or other overseas people. This was one of the challenges Millicent Iton had to take up when she became director of CANSAVE.

> Some people said, 'oh, it wouldn't last, now that the white people have gone.' And so I had to prove to myself and to others as well, that local people, Black people, can manage things and if we are sure of what we are doing we can do very well if not better.

There is no question that CANSAVE is better or that it has grown. One of the first things that she did when she took charge was a reorientation in the teacher training program.

> I introduced a couple of new courses. One was the sociology of the Caribbean family, we didn't have any course on sociology before. I think people need to know their origins and to understand too what was happening in the family and the behaviour of our children. If they were able to understand a little bit of our Caribbean family structure, then they would be better able to understand the children and their needs.

Teaching, child rearing, nutrition, teacher education and nursery schools have always been activities in which women have been involved. It is no surprise then that CANSAVE's staff is dominated by women and run by women, and Millicent Iton has tried to create an awareness in the organization that women are important.

> One of the things I know I have worked hard on, is to inject a consciousness of women, and their potential, and what they are capable of doing. I think this is part of the secret of whatever success there is in CANSAVE.

Being in charge of CANSAVE requires an ability to make tough decisions. Because it is an organization in the business of helping people, there have to be decisions concerning what is help and what is not. It is important to distinguish between help that is charity and help that contributes to self-reliance and independence rather than dependence.

> I go all the way to help people who need help. I just don't hand out. As you help, you have to help to educate, you have to help them to see why they are being helped. But you have to point out that help does not go on forever. You have to help people to self-sufficiency.

There is always the concern for balance, between helping and hindering, between being in charge and being part of a team. These are the issues that Millicent Iton constantly grapples with in running her organization.

She has been a teacher, a civil servant, a housewife and director of CANSAVE. She would like to see the organization train more young people with a professional outlook on child development. She would like to see more indigenous material created for teaching and training purposes and to initiate a systematic process of documentation of successful programs. CANSAVE, she feels, should become more involved with adolescents because their needs are being neglected. Her contribution to her society has been primarily through this organization. Teachers have been trained, women have been involved in self-help programs, and hundreds have had their first exposure to education through her programs. She has shown that a woman and a Vincentian could run an organization as efficiently as the British or Canadians. Millicent Iton is a tall distinguished woman with gray hair. Some people describe her as having a purposeful walk. She describes herself as a "no nonsense woman" who has:

> dedication to duty. If I am doing something I am doing it with heart and soul, no half-way measures. I have a great sense of trust, I think I have a sense of intuition and I know people. I have a sense of humility and I know my limitations. I respect other people and I respect myself. What I strive to get women to do is recognize their potential and use it for their own development. I think that in our own society, they have been always playing second fiddle. We cannot lag behind men. The

men are doing some things but the men haven't got all the answers. There are two sexes and we must work together. Women themselves must learn to unite, and be kinder to one another. If we put a high value on ourselves then we can unite and not allow others to take advantage of us.

In 1983 she left CANSAVE to work with UNICEF. Through this organization based in St. Vincent she has been able to share her experience with the region. She has written a training manual, *Training for Nursery Workers*, developed Caribbean material for nursery school teachers and conducted many workshops in the training of teachers.

This has been one of her dreams in her field of early childhood education – the development of indigenous material for teaching and training purposes.

When she was a little girl she read a lot and dreamt a lot. She believes that dreams are important. Everyone should have a dream.

Whatever you do, set high standards and set out to achieve them. I used to dream a lot as a girl and I still have dreams. I feel that one needs to have dreams come true. If you aim at the sky and you get to the tree top then you're never too low.

Ann Liburd

December 12, 1920
President, Caribbean Women's Association
St. Kitts

The capital of St. Kitts is Basseterre, a small charming city with narrow picturesque streets. The buildings are old quaint wooden structures with jalousie windows and large spaces. On Central Street there is a small shop called the Specialty Shop. Here one can find a little of everything; colognes, the latest thing in blouses and handbags, shampoos and biscuits. One can also get freshly made "mauby" and ginger beer and Ms. Liburd's coconut cake. Such a shop used to be called a "cake shop" — a place where one can buy some essentials, sit and drink mauby or a cold drink, have a piece of cake and chat.

This is Ms. Liburd's shop. It is one of the fun places to be. Ms. Liburd is entertaining and assertive. She sits behind her counter, chatting with her customers.

> Mornin Ms. Liburd, you get that new shoes yet?
> No darlin, I going Puerto Rico to buy next week, I will get some nice shoes then.
> O.K. Ms. Liburd, I going come back
> O.K. darlin.

Ann Liburd earns her living by running this small shop. She goes to Puerto Rico several times a year on buying trips. In St. Kitts, most of the small vendoring businesses, be they shops like Ms. Liburd's or stalls in the market, are run by women. In this respect, Ann Liburd shares an occupation common to many Caribbean women. Going to the "Specialty Shop" watching the shopkeeper selling her goods, chatting with people about politics, about church, about cooking, about the latest marriage or birth, one would sense a warm and special person. Certainly one would have little inkling that Ann Liburd is a force to be reckoned with. She is a dynamo at conferences and meetings, she is an outstanding speaker and preacher, well-travelled, three times president of the Caribbean Women's Association, the president of the National Council of Women in St. Kitts and creator or member of several other women's organizations.

Ms. Liburd's whole life has been in service to other women. In many ways these involvements are typical of what women have traditionally done. There have long been women's organizations, like the Toast Mistress Club, 4-H Parent Clubs, church women's groups and various kinds of women's social groups. These groups however are not seen as organizations of great political power or effectiveness in larger society.

This view of traditional women's organizations is only a stereotype. It is true that these organizations held little political or economic power, but they fulfilled a great need. It was in these organizations that women took on formal leadership roles. It was here that they became exposed to, and generated new ideas on child rearing, cooking, managing their families and making miniscule budgets stretch. It was through these organizations that women raised money to build and equip schools and churches.

And yet, these women's organizations were viewed as frivolous. Women themselves often saw their activities as marginal to the important work of running and maintaining a population. "She is *just* a housewife," "she is *only* the children's mother," "She *just* sells in the market," and "it's one of those *women's* organizations — you know how they are." There is always an element of condescension. Women have been discriminated against and their work devalued for a variety of reasons. Women are supposed to be selfless and not interested in personal gain. One rationalization for paying women a lower wage is that they do not need that much money because their husbands are supporting them, and their income is supplementary, a little extra money for the home. This is a myth. Women are quite often the sole breadwinner in their families, particularly in an island like St. Kitts where 46% of the households are headed by women.

Women's organizations have been seen as an activity for a particular class. Nice upper-class ladies who have nothing better to do but occupy themselves with volunteer work. Some women's organizations may fall into this category, but what is true is that 4-H parent clubs and women's church groups like the Mother's Union are not merely pastimes for the well off. Ann Liburd's participation is an example of this.

Ann Liburd was born on December 12, 1920 in Antigua. Her mother was a washerwoman and her father a farmer. Her mother was a strict woman who believed in education. Ann finished high school and passed her Senior Cambridge. Her ambition was to teach, which she did briefly. She considers herself a Kittitian, because she spent most of her adult life there. She married a Kittitian and moved to St. Kitts in 1946. In many ways Ann Liburd's life runs the gamut of traditional women's jobs. She was in the St. Kitts civil service as secretary to the education officer; she retired and used her gratuity to open the "Specialty Shop". She has always been a strong church woman, worked tirelessly for women's organizations, and is the mother of six children.

Ms. Liburd has gained her leadership and visibility in St. Kitts by excelling at each of these activities. Her connection to the church is pivotal. She has been a lay preacher and a member of the church board. All of these activities, the church, the women's organizations, and the shop are geared towards her work with women. In each arena, Ann is an example of how a traditional female activity can become a power base for women's own self-preservation. As a mother, she has contributed lawyers, a teacher and a politician to her society. She uses this access to skills to facilitate services to women and their families on the island — invaluable on a small island with limited resources. As a church member she again redefines that traditional involvement for women by taking on the responsibility of being a lay preacher and involving herself in the decision-making process of the church. As a shopkeeper, another typical female activity, she becomes entrepreneur not only for goods, but for local products. She ensures that her shop sells mauby, tamarind and sorrel drinks and cakes of all local derivation. These are all directly related to her women's organization activities. Here she provides the women who make these items with a ready market and at the same time promotes local culture.

This is another unrecognized activity of women's organizations. The use of indigenous fruit and vegetables has been a major economic and cultural enterprise for small developing countries whose only resources are local products and skills. Women in these organizations started years ago to experiment with and create local products which would benefit first their own families and their budgets, but which in the long run, benefitted both the larger economy and cultural character of their societies. Finally Ann's goal within various women's organizations is to teach women skills for self-employment.

> Women are the hewers of wood and the carriers of water. Many times when I was teaching in the country I would see women, pregnant women, their belly near to touch their mouths, with a buckets of water on their heads and de potato and so in their hands, you know, and my heart would go out to them. In the sun you see them going. In St. Kitts most households are headed by women. I don't know, it is a Caribbean thing, but you know, it made an impression on me, that the women were neglected, you know women were not taken care of. And even husbands and wives in good homes, the woman was taken as a piece of furniture.

Ann Liburd, like Didi, is an activist. She acts when she sees injustice. No one would describe her as shy and retiring. She is a tall, striking woman, ebullient and articulate. She loves music and is a great storyteller. What makes her an effective leader is that her various activities keep her in touch with the woman who is struggling to make it. She listens, observes and talks to the women.

> Well tell me man, what happenin with the children?
> Ms. Liburd, the big girl with child. She have to leave school. I don't know what to do Ms. Liburd, I thought she would be different.

At a conference in Barbados or in the United States, Ann Liburd would translate these conversations.

> The women in our island are burdened by two things. One is the number of children that they must raise. These children are not only their own children, but their grandchildren. This means that their money cannot stretch far enough. The other problem is the high level of teenage pregnancies.

One minute Ann can be talking to a rural woman about her problems and, in the next, to a representative from an international organization about the same issues. It is a skill that is essential to solving women's problems or the community's problems in general. This is at the core of the process of representing the people. It is fitting that she was elected by Caribbean women to be president of the Caribbean Women's Association three times. The Caribbean Women's Association is an umbrella organization for over 500 women's organizations in the region. Ann Liburd was their first president. The women elected her because they were affected by her dynamism, her articulateness and her genuine concern for the welfare of women. She transforms traditional women's roles and activities into arenas of power, self-esteem and integrity. This she does by restructuring the perceptions of what women do.

> I believe not in superiority but in equality. If you are going to play domino, and draughts and bridge and you have you night out, a woman should have her night out too. When she stays up with the children when they are sick and you don't stay w;th them, well some of them say that's woman's work. But I believe that women have too long been in the background, and they must come to the fore. In all the population of the

Caribbean, especially in St. Kitts, women are more than men. Politicians all the time get up and say they are going to take the country 'forward' and 'progress'. You just progress with the minority and leave the majority behind? In parliament — men make all the decisions for you.

Women have always done meaningful things. Both women themselves and society have devalued women's work. Ann values herself and tries to help other women value their labour. Ann Liburd looks around her and sees the everyday activities of her society, but she has the eye of a woman who sees the power and beauty in other women.

I see a woman whose husband works in the mountain in the Malineaux estate about eight miles from town. And she only go up in the mountain to help him bring food down. But she sells it in the market every Saturday. And when she finish selling in the market, she walk around and she buy the food, the relish they call it, the meat that is necessary for next week, because she is going to have all the potatoes and breadfruit and maybe a little rice and so forth with it. The other day, I saw her in town, and she said, 'Well, you know, I have a little money and I'm going down here to the lumber yard,' because she want to put another little bit on the house, and nobody can pay her to do that. The woman is a born economist. You know she don't have no Ph.D. in economics, but she is a born economist.

This is what I see.

Women in Politics

Controversial because they have power and have taken a stand, Mary Eugenia Charles, Mary Margaret Dyer-Howe, Shirley Field-Ridley and Phyllis Shand Allfrey have been women of significance because of their acquisition of political power.

In Caribbean history, women have been involved in politics, but only at a very low level. They attend meetings, raise funds for the party and work for their parties and candidates tirelessly. Yet it has been rare for a woman to be party chairman, prime minister or minister of government. Women, while important to the political system, rarely wield power themselves.

The achievements of the women in this section then, must be regarded in this context. One of the objectives here is to recognize Phyllis Shand Allfrey and her contribution not only to Dominica, but to the Caribbean. *The Orchid House* should become one of the books read in schools as it is a view of life in the Caribbean that has rarely been written about; and one that no longer exists.

Both Mary Dyer-Howe and Shirley Field-Ridley struggled tirelessly for women's rights. They brought to their ministries a concern and a sensitivity about the status of women. These two women have symbolized the ideal new woman — a woman who had achieved a position of power while at the same time maintaining a sensitivity to the needs of women in their societies.

The women in this section represent the major political currents in the Caribbean. In Montserrat, Mary Margaret Dyer-Howe, the Minister of Education, is involved in a political system very strongly connected to England. Shirley Field-Ridley was involved in the government of Forbes Burnham in Guyana. Phyllis Shand Allfrey and Mary Eugenia Charles, both Dominican women, also represent two important streams of politics in the region. In her day, Phyllis Shand Allfrey was a socialist. Eugenia Charles, one of the few female prime ministers in the world, is a firm ally of the United States, as shown in her support of their invasion of Grenada.

These are the rare women who have gained access to power traditionally held by men. Women having political power is a relatively new feature of our societies and both the people and the women themselves of this region must become adjusted to this. Jackie Creft, minister of government under Maurice Bishop in Grenada, was among the group of his strongest allies who was killed. Phyllis Shand Allfrey gave her all for Dominica and died in penury. But the risks of politics are serious for both men and women. Phyllis Shand Allfrey and Shirley Field-Ridley both of whom are dead, have left their mark on the history of the Caribbean and their countries. Mary Eugenia Charles and Mary Margaret Dyer-Howe are still influencing events in their region and their countries.

Phyllis Shand Allfrey

October 25, 1908 — February 6, 1986
Dominica
Minister of the Federal Government of the
West Indies
1958-1962

The Caribbean is populated by people of many races; Europeans, East Indians, Amerindians, Caribs, Africans and Chinese. Although it is an area of largely African descent, each race is significant even though their numbers may be small. The

Amerindians and Caribs are small in number but they are extremely important because they are the indigenous people of this region. The Chinese are also small in number but significant in countries like Jamaica, Trinidad and Guyana. There are large numbers of people of East Indian descent living in Guyana and Trinidad. Perhaps the most powerful population in the region has been the European or white population. Although small in number, they have been the colonizers of this region.

As the history of this region evolved, the white person moved from a position of power and wealth that was visible to one that was invisible. This happened as the local populations of the region became conscious of race and ethnicity; and of the inequalities which at that time meant that if you were Black you were inferior and poor and if you were white you were privileged and wealthy. The white person became a symbol of all that oppressed us and in trying to take control of our own destinies we had to separate ourselves from this white domination.

This preamble is important to an understanding of Phyllis Shand Allfrey. She died on February 6, 1986 virtually unheralded and unhailed. The New Chronicle, Dominica's main newspaper, described her passing thus: "She died in solitude and grief — just a frail old lady, yet the outside world hails her as being one of the Caribbean's most prominent politicians in her time."

The Orchid House, which is the story of a white elite family during the colonial period in Dominica, is Phyllis Allfrey's family biography centred around their home L'Aromatique. The story is told through Lally the black nurse maid. Lally was always concerned about Joan, whose life in the book mirrors Phyllis Allfrey's own early political life. Phyllis Allfrey returned to Dominica in 1953 having lived in London the life of a liberal socialist, and having returned she met Mr. Loblack the union organizer. He and Ms. Allfrey waged the early struggles to establish the labour party and campaigned among the plantation workers. The decision to stand up against the injustices suffered by the poor and black in Dominica was a risk for Phyllis Allfrey both among her own people and among the black workers themselves. Imagine the commotion, the sight that this white woman and black man caused as they walked through the plantations trying to organize.

The following excerpts from *The Orchid House* provide a glimpse of Joan's and Baptiste's (in the role of Mr. Loblack) political struggles.

> The lime-oil factory was in sight. A sound of machinery and a heightened citron smell told them that they had arrived at the boundary of the town. Cauldron-like puffs of steaming smoke evaporated in the bright air. A little gang of labourers with baskets of limes on their heads were passing through a gate. They stood still to gaze, and some of them greeted Baptiste, who waved and muttered embarrased words. The others started laughing and speaking patios: she caught the jeering words "Backra" and "Negre". "Never mind, they don't know that I understand, perhaps they don't even know who I am," said Joan serenly. "Oh yes, Miss Joan - they know who you are." "They must get used to seeing us together. After all, they are the people I've come to help." (p.144)

Phyllis Shand Allfrey was born in Dominica on October 25, 1908. She was the founder of the Labour Party with E.C. Loblack and a founder with Eugenia Charles and others of the Dominica Freedom Party. She was the only female cabinet minister of The West Indies Federation, the editor of the Dominica Herald newspaper and then later edited her own newspaper, *The Star;* the author of a prize winning collection of poems, *Palm and Oak* and author of *The Orchid House,* a book which is now highly regarded in literary circles after being out of print for some years. She was a politician, a journalist, a poet and novelist. She was one of the outstanding women of the Caribbean and certainly an outstanding Dominican.

Phyllis Allfrey and E.C. Loblack went on to challenge the government by running for elections in 1957. Mr. Loblack won his seat but Phyllis Allfrey, although very popular, did not. In 1958 the Dominican Labour Party allied itself with the West Indies Labour Party which ran for elections throughout the region to form the Federation of the West Indies. E.C. Loblack and Phyllis Shand Allfrey stood for the election as the two representatives for Dominica in the Federal government. Phyllis Allfrey won by amassing the greatest number of votes, more than Mr. Loblack himself. Before the election, she was in England on a business trip and had to rush back to Dominica to stand for the Federal election.

Reaching Barbados she hitched a lift on a Geest banana boat to Dominica and she landed on the quay with a straw hat pulled down over her face, clutching precious printed election leaflets. The first thing she heard was the market woman saying the white woman promised to come back and she didn't come. "I lifted my hat from my face and said in Patois 'moi vee way'. I have arrived. I felt as if I had already won." (Pattullo, Caribbean Chronicle).

She was appointed by Sir Grantley Adams head of the Federation Government as Minister for Labour and Social Affairs, the only female cabinet minister of the Federal government. She held this portfolio for four years until the Federation collapsed in 1962. The four years outside of Dominica had kept her out of touch with the people. E.C. Loblack has resigned earlier from the Federation and returned home. During the early Sixties the political environment was heavily influenced by McCarthyism. Joseph McCarthy was an American politician who was suspicious of anyone who criticised the system. They were accused of being anti-American and therefore communist. Many people were arrested and investigated during this time. This "McCarthy" attitude strongly influenced politics in the Caribbean and Phyllis Allfrey's own socialist orientation made her extremely vulnerable. She then became a liability to her party. As the Labour Party grew in popularity and black consciousness began to emerge in the 1960s, Phyllis Allfrey, though still popular among the people, became a white person, a white woman and a socialist from whom the party wanted to distance themselves.

When she returned to Dominica, she was out of work. Her husband had earlier lost his job at the L. Rose Company because of her political activities. She then took the editorship of the "Dominica Herald" newspaper, which she subsequently lost because of an editorial in the Herald which criticized a banana export tax. This criticism was then used as the reason to expel her from the Labour Party. This was a great blow to her, for she had given her all to the party. She had lost her ties with the white elite because of her socialist political activities and the Labour Party which she founded no longer wanted her.

In 1965 she started her own newspaper called *The Star*. This newspaper was both political and literary and many young writers in Dominica were first published here. By this time, Phyllis Allfrey had hardly any money; her family had sold off their properties. She spent most of her money on publishing *The Star* and lived on her husband's small savings.

In 1968 the government tried to pass a bill, an amendment to the Seditious and Undesirable Publications Act. This would have effectively muzzled freedom of speech. Phyllis Allfrey rounded up other editors and formed a group who went throughout the island speaking out against this act. One of this group was Eugenia Charles who emerged as the leader and later prime minister of Dominica. At the start the group was called the freedom fighters and in October 1968; the Dominica Freedom Party was formed with Phyllis Allfrey as one of the founding members. Her newspaper, *The Star*, then became the organ of the Freedom Party and once more she invested her pennies and efforts in this cause. Now she stood up against the Labour Party which she had formed.

This, of course, made her life socially and financially difficult. From 1968 to 1978 she struggled with *The Star*. By 1982, (by which time the Freedom Party was in power), she had ended its publication. Her only recognition from the new government was the Golden Drum Award which was given to her by the Cultural Division for her encouragement to young people through *The Star* in their literary development.

Phyllis Allfrey spent her last years in poverty. She was deeply attached to her husband who became ill and for whom she cared till the day she died. She had five children, two of her own a son and a daughter who died in 1977, and three adopted Carib children, one of whom, David, took care of her in her last days.

Phyllis Allfrey believed in the equality of the races and in the dignity of the human being regardless of colour. Her life was caught up in the politics of transition — the period in this region when there was a shift from white to black rule and a growing black elite. She was white, she was a woman, and she was from an elitist background. She was a socialist who took the risk of standing up for her convictions regardless of whether the government was black or white. These things prevented others from seeing her as another Dominican, another West Indian committed to her country and her people.

This woman who was born to wealth in Dominica died in penury; this woman who founded the Labour Party and also the Freedom Party was virtually ignored by these parties. She was the only female minister of the Federation government, and one of the great women of Dominica and the West Indies. Dominica is known internationally for three women: Eugenia Charles, the Prime Minister; Jean Rhys, the writer; and Phyllis Allfrey, the author of *The Orchid House*. Yet few people in Dominica have read *The Orchid House*. She was an idealist and as she said in that book, "Idealists seem to attract indirect persecution."

She loved Dominica, the hills, the trees, the flora, the fauna and the sun. She had a boyish charm, blue eyes, blond hair and was 'straight and quick.' Lennox Honeychurch, the Dominican historian who was apprenticed to her for many years on *The Star,* remembered her this way:

> She was passionate about Dominica and had a love for all these islands and was a great romantic. The struggle was a great romance for her. Towards the end, particularly one of the things that personally hurt me, people did not, and it hurt her a great deal too, people did not look back. They did not give her the support or the sympathy that I think she deserved.

Phyllis Shand Allfrey was a great Dominican, her life so full of irony and tragedy has yet to be seriously examined in this region. She sacrificed her literary career and her own well-being for the struggle in Dominica. It was a struggle that made her life more difficult than easy, but she didn't mind because it was what she wanted. If the young Phyllis Allfrey were to be presented with a view of what her life would become she might have said exactly what she wrote in *The Orchid House:* "Oh Lally, even if the sparkle of the sea hurts my eyes, I want to see it. I don't mind being hurt."

Margaret Mary Dyer-Howe

November 18, 1940
Minister of Education
Montserrat

Montserrat is a small island twenty-seven miles north west of Antigua with a population of twelve thousand. It is known as the "Emerald Isle" because of its overwhelmingly deep, rich green appearance. The mat of green vegetation wraps itself around the three groups of mountains which jut out dramatically making the name Montserrat (jagged ridge) apt.

Margaret Mary Dyer-Howe was born in St. Patrick on the island of Montserrat on the 18th of November, 1940. She became the only female member of parliament in 1979 and 3 years later was made minister of Education. She was raised by her grandmother who was a farmer and a midwife.

> I was raised by my grandmother and I look up to her because she was a woman of strength. She was a community woman, she was a district midwife. She was a role model for me. A lot of people say I take after her. I would have liked to know that she would be around to see me today because she always figure that because I didn't have this farming inclination that I wouldn't be able to make it in life. She was a farmer and she figured that you had to do this in order to get a livelihood and she couldn't see anything beyond that, so I really would have liked her to see me today and to see my achievements. I tried to work the hoe, but I just couldn't negotiate the thing. I tried but I couldn't do anything in that line, I just can't.

Margaret Dyer-Howe did not go to high school because it was too expensive: high schools were not free when she was growing up. After she left primary school, she was sent to learn sewing, a typical pursuit for young women at that time. This was followed by studying for her teacher's certificate and teaching third grade in primary school.

The opportunity to go abroad came up through an uncle who lived in the United States. She did go to the United States and took a one-year course in secretarial training and then returned to Montserrat where she worked as a secretary, first in the private sector and then in government. Meanwhile, she married her first husband, a member of parliament who died several years ago. While he was alive she left her secretarial work to run his business. It was during this time that she became involved in several community organizations: the Social League, a women's organization, the Old People's Welfare Association and the St. Patrick's Credit Union. She also became the president of the Social League.

Although her community work was mostly concentrated on women and the elderly, she also served the community in many other capacities. After several years in her husband's business, she decided to return to her secretarial work, becoming secretary of the island's Water Authority. Soon she was promoted to executive officer and then adminstrative officer — the head of the Water Authority.

She continued her involvement with the Social League and the Old People's Association. It was at this time that she initiated the Social League Garment project which in 1985 was one of the projects chosen for an award at the Honours ceremony of the Decade of Women Conference in Nairobi.

The decision to enter politics was not an easy one. She was asked to run for the seat in her community not only by members of her party but by members of the community.

> I saw the opportunity for a position for a female politician in the house and I simply took hold of the opportunity. The former administration had a female minister and I thought that by going into politics and holding this seat it would be a continuation of the progress of women in politics. It would also encourage other women to have a female figure in politics. It was not an easy decision for me to go into politics.

Many Caribbean people first get involved in politics at the community level. They build a reputation as concerned citizens at the local level. Although women are very active in their communities, like Ms. Pascal or Nurse Baptiste, they very rarely use that credibility to start a career in politics.

When she became Minister of Education, Health, Community Service and Women's Affairs, Margaret Dyer-Howe had a very clear agenda:

> I wanted to restructure the educational system because the system was unfair and not relevant to our own needs. The common entrance exam is set in such a way that only a limited number of children can pass. Middle-class and upper-class children had a better chance of passing because their parents could pay to have their children tutored. I think this system should be changed to allow every child a chance at secondary education. We need as many educated people as possible, not just a few highly educated. Of course, making this change is not easy but I will do it.

Being a politician, a woman, and a woman interested in improving the status of women, can be a difficult task, for a lot of convincing and politicking is necessary to bring about the recognition that laws, structures and mechanisms are needed to integrate women fully in the development process. The recognition of the unequal status of women is not immediately apparent because those in power are not women and sex discrimination, if not directly experienced, is often difficult for those who are not discriminated against to understand. As well, some women who have gained status and success do not see this discrimination. This is largely because they themselves have had more freedom to do what they wanted. This does not mean that discrimination does not exist, it means that those particular women were able to succeed.

Margaret Dyer-Howe is an unusual women because she has made it in a male field and continues to understand the barriers women face. She does not separate herself from the discrimination other women face because she was able to succeed. She remembers her own obstacles and tries to support and encourage other women to overcome them too. Women can now file their taxes separately from their husbands; the word "illegitimate", which was once put on the birth certificates of children born out of wedlock, has now been deleted. Previously if a non-Montserratian woman married a man born in Montserrat, the woman could acquire belonger status. A Monserratian woman however was not entitled to this right, if she married a non-Monserratian. This is now changed, both men and women from Montserrat can gain belonger status for their spouses if they so wish. Margaret Dyer-Howe was instrumental in bringing about the status changes.

M.P. Margaret Mary Dyer is a tall, lovely women. She is accessible and responsive. She has a knack with people, particularly the elderly for whom she has a soft spot. Her personality is marked by warmth and intelligence and caring. She is a woman who is dedicated and very serious about being a politician. This is a woman who did not go to high school, who was sent to learn to sew, who was a secretary and who was the only female Minister in her government. Being in politics is often very controversial but Margaret Dyer-Howe believes that one should follow one's conviction.

Call it self-pride if you wish. I always think there is room for improvement in my own development process. It is important to have self-will and discipline. Discipline yourself to become what you want in life. A lot of people, close relatives of mine, told me that I should not become involved in politics and I said I must do something on my own. I have to do it on my own and not because somebody said yes or no. Most of the things I do, I do this way. They are not always right, but confidence in yourself is very important.

She has remarried and receives a great deal of emotional and moral support from her husband. Being a politician in a small island can be difficult and lonely and it is the people at such times who renew her spirit and commitment.

I have a good relationship with a lot of people and especially the older people, and they would say, 'oh, you're doing a good job. We appreciate what you're doing. If we had one or two more like you things would have been better.'
When I get worried that things are not moving the way I want them to, I am comforted by the thought that there is somebody out there who appreciates what I do.

Mary Eugenia Charles

May 15, 1919
Prime Minister
Dominica

M ary Eugenia Charles is the Caribbean's first female prime minister. Born in the village of Pointe Michel in Dominica on the 15th of May, 1919, she has scored a number of firsts. Her parents, a mason and a launderer, were determined that she and her two brothers would be educated. They became doctors and she a lawyer. She was the first female Dominican lawyer in her country, the first to have her own practice and the first female opposition leader in the Caribbean and in Dominica.

Her interest in law came out of her training in shorthand and typing.

> My father insisted that I take shorthand and typing before I
> took my 'O' levels. So I passed my shorthand and typing
> before my 'O' levels and I wanted to keep it up, so I used to
> go to courts when I was off on holidays to practice. I got in-
> terested in the law because I used to be in the courts practic-
> ing my shorthand. The person who influenced me most was
> Judge Malone. He was a lawyer at the time and there was
> quite a famous case we had here to do with a will and I was
> so fascinated with the way he conducted this case I felt that
> this was for me.

> Immediately after leaving high school, she went to Canada
> to take up law. She attended the University of Toronto and ob-
> tained her B.A. in 1945. In 1947, she was called to the Bar in
> London and returned to Dominica in 1949. The time she spent
> abroad was very satisfying.

> I loved it, I loved it, but I was always very conscious though
> that I was living an artificial life, because I was living on cam-
> pus. I recognized that I didn't have to shovel snow, I didn't
> have to worry about the thermostat, we were really cared for.

However, her sojourn abroad was not without incident. While
in the U.S.A., she experienced racial discrimination and one particular incident in Detroit, Michigan, outraged her. She was
refused entry into a a a restaurant by the maitre d' and immediately
brought charges against the man. In the preliminary hearing
before the judge she said:

> This man must be punished. Make him understand that he
> can't do this. He must lose his job. I want that man punished.
> He has broken your law, you say your country believes in law
> and order. He is a criminal. He must be punished. I am not
> going to have it. I come from a country where people are
> black and people are respected for being black and I am not
> going to come to this two-by-four country and have anyone
> treat me this way.

When she returned to Dominica in 1949 she immediately
opened up her own practice. This same outspokenness thrust
her into politics and made her name as a lawyer. She ran the office alone, doing all the jobs herself. After six months she was
able to hire a clerk and soon had a practice large enough to re-

quire the services of five clerks. Most of her practice was focused on property law.

> I liked doing the research. I liked finding out the background on something and looking up old documents. It was a nice tidy thing. When it was complete you know it's done.

Her career and contribution as a lawyer was marked by another first. She was the first lawyer to file a *habeas corpus* in Dominica. A *habeas corpus* is a document that protects a person from illegal imprisonment. This writ requires that the person either be brought to court to face legal charges or be set free.

> The first thing I did in the high court was a *habeas corpus* which had never been done in Dominica before. There was no precedent for it, so I had to start from scratch looking into the books to find the precedent. I went before Justice Crane who was from Guyana. At first when I tried to file it the registrar said that it was wrong. So I went back and put down page and paragraph and why I was doing it because I had to convince myself that I was right. I went back to him and I said, 'I'm sorry, I think that I am right. Could you please file it.' I went before Justice Crane and his first thought was that I hadn't done the right procedure. So I said, 'Sir, if you'll hear me on this.' It was a good thing that I had gone back and checked because of the registrar. After I was through he said, 'Yes, you're right, this is the procedure, but in Guyana we do it differently.' I think it was the first *habeas corpus,* certainly in living memory, in Dominica.

Having worked in law for many years, she became aware of inequities in the law in regards to women. However, her practice was a general one and, as a rule, did not focus on women specifically.

> I feel the law should be changed that when there is a divorce, the woman should be entitled to half of the property. This was not so in Dominica. The woman had to make a claim to show that she had contributed to the accumulation of property. Like my father always said, without my mother, he would never have achieved what he did, because although she didn't go out and work, she saved, and she encouraged him and assisted him. So he always felt that the property was equally hers and his. We have a law that a woman who has a child out of wedlock could go to court and prove who the father is

and an award is made for the father to pay child support. We
think the current payment is very low and has to be
increased.

While building up her practice, Eugenia Charles was also
writing articles in the newspaper regularly. She was outspoken
and critical of many government policies. The government tried
to pass a bill, an amendment to the Seditious and Undesirable
Publications Act.

In its draft wording, it would have prevented an opposition
party from existing.

There was a great deal of protest over this bill and Ms. Charles'
voice was one of the most vociferous. As a result, she and several
others including Phyllis Shand Allfrey formed the Freedom Party
in 1968. At a huge public meeting protesting the bill she made
her first political speech. She and other members had organized
a demonstration against this bill and they sent in a petition
demanding the bill's repeal.

It was at this time that the Premier said, 'we are here to rule
and rule we will.' Then I decided that we had to get them out.
It took us twelve years, but we did it.

With the birth of the Freedom Party, Eugenia Charles was
launched into politics proper. She ran unsuccessfully for her first
seat in 1970. However, she took her place in Parliament as a
nominated member. In 1975, she was elected representative for
Roseau and became official leader of the opposition. The
Freedom Party continued to struggle and in 1980, under Eugenia
Charles' leadership, they won seventeen of the twenty-one seats
in the House of Assembly in the general elections. It was then
that she became Prime Minister, after having been in politics for
only twelve years. When they won the elections she was, of
course, very happy.

I was glad that we won because we worked so hard for twelve
years. I was glad also because I felt that at last we could do
something about what was happening in the country. Being
Prime Minister means a lot of hard work, a lot of hard work.
But really I don't think it makes any difference to me that I
am Prime Minister. I don't think I live any differently, I live

just my simple life as usual. There is more traveling and I have to go places because it is important to what we are doing. But I'd rather sit at home and read a book, frankly.

The government of Eugenia Charles was elected for a second term and Ms. Charles has become well known not only regionally but internationally as well.

There is nothing that could stop a woman, a coloured woman, a woman born in a small country, from doing the things she wants to do and reaching the top.

Perhaps the most important event in triggering her international recognition was the U.S. intervention in Grenada in 1983. Eugenia Charles was among those heads of government who supported the U.S., and was perhaps the most visible of these supporters to be associated with this event as she accompanied the U.S. president Ronald Reagan when he informed the international press of the U.S. invasion of Grenada.

Within the region there has been a great deal of controversy over the U.S. invasion of Grenada and the continuing U.S. presence. Those against the invasion hold that the U.S. involvement was a violation of international law, and that Eugenia Charles and those other Caribbean heads of government who supported the Grenada intervention have betrayed the sovereignty of the region and Grenada. They argue that this support for the American invasion provided legitimacy for an act which the U.S. would have done anyway, and made the U.S. look good.

Those who supported the U.S. invasion of Grenada have argued that Grenada was in chaos and that the population was in great fear over the house arrest of Maurice Bishop and his subsequent death and the deaths of other ministers of government. They argue that the only thing to be done was for the U.S. to use its strength to "rescue" the people from this fear and chaos. Is it then to be assumed that the people of the region cannot solve their own problems? This debate is not easily resolved.

It is a different day for Eugenia Charles in Dominica. The days when she was the opposition, when she and the Freedom Party struggled for a place are gone. Now there is opposition to her government. In the end the power lies with the people, for it is they who will decide who governs.

Ms. Charles has been criticized for being cold, hard, manlike and unfeeling. She never allowed such accusations to undermine her beliefs.

> I don't really care what they say. I know where I am going. I know what I am made of. A lot of women wouldn't take part because of such abuse. I say to women forget about it and just go ahead and do the work you have to do.

Shirley Field-Ridley

August 24, 1937 — June 30, 1983
Politician
Guyana

I n the mid 1800s, the planters in the colony of British Guiana
needed to provide their children with a secondary education
in the colony rather than sending them off to England. In 1844,
the Bishop of Guiana, with financial support from the plantocracy,
established the Queen's College Grammar School. This was an
all-boys school. Bishop's High School, an all-girls school, was
started a few years later.

These schools in theory were open to all classes and races,
but the children of poor people could not enter them because
of high fees, while those whose parents could pay were
debarred through circumstances of illegitimate birth or religion
or both.[1]

Shirley Field-Ridley attended Bishop's High School in the 1950s. It was still an elitist institution. Most of the students came from rich families of affluence and privilege. Shirley was one of the first in a group of students from poor families to gain entrance into Bishop's High School. She was able to do this by winning a scholarship in a Nationwide competitive examination. The academic level at Bishop's was an easy one for her to maintain, for she was unquestionably bright and talented. But she came from a struggling family of seven children, and for an adolescent young woman becoming aware of herself and the world around her, the difference between herself and her peers at Bishop's was a little overwhelming. They knew what teachers expected of them and they changed their uniforms regularly, because they had more than one.

This environment made Shirley feel unsure of herself. Exactly how was one supposed to behave, speak and look? If she were at home or in her old school she would know because everyone valued the same things. They knew how to communicate with one another, they dressed similarly and had common problems. But Bishop's High School was a new and different experience.

Here one got the best secondary education the country could provide. It was an honour for a child from a poor family to attend Bishop's High School. For a child unaccustomed to high society this honour carried with it a great deal of anxiety. "Many people do not know this about me but I had a very hard time at Bishop's. It was a very traumatic experience for me."

In the end she prevailed and did not allow the difference to intimidate her. One of the ways she coped was by involving herself with a group of girls who were from a similar background. They formed a little group and gave each other moral support. It was a haven in which they could relax and be themselves. Soon she became familiar with, and at ease in this environment. It was a lesson that increased her political awareness of herself and her status, and a lesson that taught her the coping skills that were to become an important part of her personality.

Shirley Field-Ridley came from a very politically conscious family. Her father was one of the original members of the People's Progressive Party which was formed in 1950 and was a candidate in the 1957 elections. He did not know it but his daughter would achieve a success in politics far beyond his own expectations. Women as candidates in elections is still not common place today by any means, but in the 1950s it was a rare phenomenon. Shirley Field-Ridley did not run for elections in the 1950s, she was at the University of the West Indies at the time, but she did take some time off to come home and campaign for her father in 1957. It should be noted here that women have always campaigned for candidates. At political meetings they will turn out en masse. They will raise money, join protest demonstrations and travel miles to support their candidates. Yet for women, this participation has not translated itself into candidacy, prime ministership, or holding ministerial positions. The presence of women in these positions is still at a token level.

She was born in Georgetown, Guyana on August 24, 1937. As she grew up, it was clear that she had a natural and quick intelligence, and what was even more evident was that she had an indomitable spirit. Her first major scholarship was the one that allowed her to attend Bishop's High School. She next won a scholarship to the University of the West Indies as a runner-up in the Guyana scholar competition. She gained her B.A. (first class honours) in history in 1958. She then went to London on a University of the West Indies scholarship to study law, and obtained her LL.B. in 1962.

After her law degree she returned to Guyana, a politically important act. Many educated Caribbean men and women never return home and the result is a shortage of skills, a "brain drain" in the home country. She had married meanwhile; her husband was politically active in Jamaica and she in Guyana. In 1968, she became a candidate for the People's National Congress in the national elections. The P.N.C. officially took over the government of Guyana in 1969, and it was then that Shirley Field-Ridley had her first ministerial post. There had been two other female ministers, Winifred Gaskin and Janet Jagan, in the previous government.

She was the new minister of education. In all she had four ministries — education, health, information and culture, and sports. This is a record for a woman in any Caribbean country. At present, each government in the Caribbean tries to have at least one minister who is female, but in the 1960s female ministers of government were practically nonexistent, and very few women ran for office. Shirley Field-Ridley was the rare woman who liked being a politician. She was not self-conscious about campaigning, speaking publicly or presenting herself as a candidate for whom one should vote.

This was certainly a long way to come for a child who was out of place in an elite high school. The path leading up to her achievements was shaped by many things. Certainly prevailing over Bishop's High School was one, and being in a political home was another. This spirit, intelligence and consciousness motivated her first political act. She felt slighted because she was born female, and she felt this injustice keenly. The first article she wrote while in school was on women.

> All these people who said that girls couldn't do this or that must be answered. I would be the one to answer them. So I took part in sports, debates or anything, so I could disprove what they said. I went to a primary school that taught us to be little ladies. They taught us exercises so our hips couldn't get too big. They taught us to cook and clean and to supervise and to embroider. They were grooming us to be the ladies of the country and ladies didn't enter into competition with men because they were somehow incapable or inferior. I couldn't buy that.

The progression of her political career started first with her taking a stand against the treatment of women as inferior. Although her career encompassed a wider political scope, the concern for the status and equality of women has always been of critical importance to her.

After eleven years as a minister, she decided in 1980 to retire from her ministerial position, and chose to return to her original campaign — the status of women. Her main focus was coordinating the women's organizations, writing a history of Guyana and raising her four children (three daughters and a son).

Some Guyanese say that her greatest contribution to Guyana was in the Venezuela border crisis of 1965. The border between Guyana and Venezuela has been disputed by the Venezuelans for over a century. The matter was apparently settled by an impartial tribunal in 1899. However, an American lawyer who had helped prepare the Venezuelan case at that time wrote a letter claiming that the tribunal acted under political pressure. This letter was published after his death in 1949. The Venezuelans used this document to reopen the border claim in 1965.

This was a serious threat and involved the movement of Venezuelan troops along the borders. The matter had to be settled both legally and historically. It was the perfect time and place for Shirley's training which was in law and history. Having the skills was, however, only part of the solution. One had to have a sense of patriotism and an astuteness to present a case that was implacable. It was done. The Venezuelans backed off reluctantly. Shirley Field-Ridley was of course not the only lawyer who worked on this assignment. It was a team effort, but she was without a doubt the star of the team and some still remember her brilliance in this assignment.

Like all political figures, Shirley Field-Ridley was a controversial figure. This is the reality of being a politician. She was a small-framed, unpretentious woman. It was rare to have a political figure acknowledged for their contributions while they are alive, because they themselves are involved in partisan politics and there are always declaimers from the opposition.

History will certainly uphold her place as one of the first Guyanese women to hold a ministerial position and the Guyanese woman who made stellar contributions at that time in alleviating the Venezuela border disputes with her country.

It was a life with great rewards, recognition, power and importance, and great risks — seeing programs or ideas die or having one's life threatened.

> I couldn't live outside Guyana. I was born in Guyana and I was raised in a family that made me conscious of the needs of the country.

For Shirley Field-Ridley consciousness translated into politics. There were disagreements, threats, acts of disrespect and hostility, which required a toughness of spirit that was acquired since the days at Bishop's High School. Shirley Field-Ridley died on June 20, 1983. She was 46 years old. Politics permeated her life. It was how she contributed to her society and it was her way of embodying what she valued most of all — being Guyanese.

[1]Vere T. Daley, *A Short History of the Guyanese People*.

Women in Public Service

The major objective in this section is to redirect the thinking about women's work which has been necessary but undervalued. Here we have a life in the civil service in Elaine Middleton, Desiree Bernard, a judge; Isabel Belgrove Sealy, a domestic; Bernice Edna Yorke, a school teacher; and Louise Rowley, Permanent Secretary. Certainly in this area Desiree Bernard is unusual not only because she is a judge, but because she is one of the few female high court judges in the region.

Domestics have been performing essential services in our societies and have educated future generations in doing this kind of work, but have not been given the respect or status that they deserve. This is not only because domestics are mainly female, but because domestic work is seen as "menial". Isabel Seely, the domestic worker profiled here, has served her own family and the family for which she worked for over forty years. It is hoped that this profile teaches the value of labour, domestic labour, and therefore erodes the elitist attitudes present among many of us towards such women and their work.

When a woman entered the Civil Service in the 1920s and 1930s, there were only three possible positions for which she qualified, none of which offered advancement beyond sorter in the Post Office. Elaine Middleton and Louise Rowley persisted in their quest for higher positions.

Louise Rowley's life provides us with a personal history of the development of the Civil Service in relation to women, and through her story we see the difficulties of a life in the Civil Service. She was ahead of her time as the first female Permanent Secretary in the Caribbean in 1956.

Judge Desiree Bernard's status as a high court judge is unusual as women in the legal profession were affected by two things; one, they entered law later than men (remember Grace Augustin of St. Lucia could not take the bar exam because she was a woman); two, they were not involved in the political process at a level that would facilitate their appointments as attorney generals or even judges in their home countries. Women have consequently been overlooked in government service and also in the legal profession.

Bernice Edna Yorke, the teacher, represents the thousands of female teachers in this region. Teachers have been overworked and underpaid and in many countries, female teachers were never made principals until recently. There were also strict rules regarding marriage and pregnancy. Teachers lost their jobs if they became pregnant and were not married and, if married, could not teach if they were pregnant. In St. Lucia in 1986, two school teachers lost their jobs because they were pregnant. As a general rule, male teachers do not lose their jobs if they have children and are not married.

It is now possible for women not only to be lawyers but to become Permanent Secretaries and to aspire to the high court judgeship of the Caribbean.

Judge Desiree Patricia Bernard

March 2, 1939
High Court Judge, Guyana

Desiree Patricia Bernard went to five primary schools. Her father was a police officer and he was often posted to various parts of the country. By the time she was eleven years old she had gone to primary schools in Georgetown, Essequibo, Albion and Plaisance. She was an only child, shy and introverted. She liked to study and was fond of reading. In her wildest imagination, she would never have guessed that she would become the first female high court judge in Guyana.

Desiree Bernard was born in Georgetown, Guyana on March 2, 1939. She, like Shirley Field-Ridley, went to Bishop's High School, after winning a government county scholarship. After leaving high school she was employed in the Guyana Civil Service. Her first ambition was to be a teacher, but this changed over time. An old school teacher suggested to her that she might pursue a law career. This was quite an unusual idea to her:

> I didn't think I had the personality for it. I was quiet and I thought lawyers had to be outspoken, and here I was a quiet person, but he said that he was thinking that I should go into the solicitor's end of it.

In Guyana and in other English colonies as well a solicitor did the background legal research for cases which barristers then presented in court. Solicitors did not perform in court, they advised clients, but more generally worked on contracts and cases. Over the years, the distinction between a barrister and solicitor became blurred and the professions were fused in Guyana in 1980. Desiree decided that this was something she should pursue. She was about to apply to the University of London for status as an external student when Norma Jackman, who became a magistrate, asked her to join a new class. On a Sunday morning in 1958, at the home of a friend, Desiree Patricia Bernard attended her first class in law.

This class consisted mostly of women who had been studying on their own but had not been very successful. At that time Fred Wills, an eminent Guyanese lawyer, had just returned from England and at their request he agreed to be their teacher.

> I discovered that I liked law. I was very fortunate to be a student of Mr. Wills. He is one of the geniuses that Guyana has produced and he made the law come alive when he lectured.

With Fred Wills as her teacher she took her first exam, the inter-L.L.B. in 1959 and passed. She wanted to try for her L.L.B. next but before she could do so she had to be articled to a practicing lawyer and was articled to Fred Wills. Becoming articled is a way of acquiring familiarity with the practice of law and knowledge of the legal profession. It gives a first-hand experience in the everyday problems and pleasures of the law profession.

She left for England in 1962 where she passed her exam and qualified as a solicitor. This took her two years to complete after which she immediately returned to Guyana. Most of Desiree Bernard's work was done as an external student. Many students who could not afford to go abroad gained their university degrees in this way. In a sense, all students who take exams that are graded in England are external students. This would include high school students who take their general certificate of education at the advanced or ordinary levels. Similarly, such a mechanism was set up with universities in England for advanced degrees like B.A.'s and inter-L.L.B.'s. For the final L.L.B. degree, residence in England was required for a short period of time. The two years that she spent in England were the only years that she lived abroad.

Law has been a profession which men traditionally pursue. Female lawyers are now quite common, but at the time Desiree Bernard started her career in law it was a field just opening up to women. After obtaining their L.L.B.'s, young lawyers began practice in various law firms. Desiree Bernard became a solicitor for the Cameron & Shephard Law firm in Georgetown after she graduated. After two years at Cameron & Shephard, she took over the practice of a colleague who was emigrating to Canada. In a short time she had become a well established lawyer with her own practice. It was rare at that time for a woman to have her own law firm.

Her practice was mostly in family law, with a focus in divorce. This made her keenly aware of the various problems men and women had to face. She was struck by the overwhelming economic pressures that women faced and the suffering this caused to the woman and her children. Desiree Bernard was particularly sensitive to these issues because of her other activities. Involved in many women's organizations, she was a founding member of the Toast Mistress Club in Guyana, and its first President in 1967. She was also active in the Business and Professional Women's Association, and C.A.S.W.I.G., the Council of Affairs on the Status of Women in Guyana. In addition, she wrote extensively on family law in Guyana.

Because of her consciousness, she has initiated major changes in the law as it affected women. Women in common-law relationships now have legal rights of inheritance of their partner's assets. Women can now file their taxes separately from their husbands, and children born to women out of wedlock have been given legal rights to inherit their father's estate.

These involvements over the years (of a highly motivated professional woman, concerned about other women, and involved in women's organizations), created an image of Desiree Bernard as a single career woman, fighting for women's rights with little interest in traditional pursuits like marriage and children. Many single women who choose to focus on their careers are often not viewed as "feminine" as other women because they did not make a husband and children their first priority. This is particularly so for women who are very successful in male dominated professions. In Desiree Bernard's case she was not only in the legal profession, but she had her own practice and was active in women's organizations. When she was approached about the judgeship in the high court, her first response was no, she did not see herself in that role — a judge was somebody older who has had many years in the profession. She joked to the Chancellor of the judiciary, "It will certainly spoil my matrimonial prospects." There is a lot of truth in this statement, not only for a judge but for many other very successful women.

In 1980 she accepted the judgeship. It was a first for a woman and a rare feat for a solicitor, male or female. Judges are not usually female in the Caribbean, or for that matter, anywhere else in the world. Desiree Bernard is the first and only woman in the high court in Guyana. There are now only a handful of women in the high court throughout the Caribbean.

Because of her visibility in women's organizations, she continued to be stereotyped as interested only in women's liberation. She wanted to change this because it was only a partial reflection of who she was. She decided therefore to concentrate on other activities and became the secretary of the Guyana Law Society. After two or three years as secretary she became the Society's president. This position led to her involvement in the Organization of the Commonwealth Caribbean Bar Association, an umbrella organization for all the Bar Associations in the region. This is, like the legal profession, a predominantly male organization. The members of this organization elected Desiree Bernard to be their president in 1976. She was the first and only female to be elected president of this august body. The only other woman who had come close to this position was Eugenia Charles who was nominated in 1972, but not elected. Desiree Bernard was shocked by her election, because she ran against an eminent St. Lucian lawyer. When the results came in, she had won by one vote.

This is a long way for a shy and quiet child to come. Today her mother and adopted daughter live with her. They provide her with the strength and support that she needs. The transition from being lawyer Bernard to Judge Bernard has not been easy. Before, when she walked to her office she would meet various colleagues and chat; now they treat her with deference. Being a judge requires circumspect and irreproachable conduct. This makes it both a responsible and a lonely position. Desiree Bernard takes law and justice seriously. All of her activities, be they as a solicitor, President of the Guyana Law Society, President of the Toast Mistress Club, student or clerical assistant in the Civil Service, are marked by a diligence and seriousness that are consistent and sustained. These are the characteristics that she has brought to her role as judge. It is important that others in the legal field perceive her as a person from whom justice can be had.

> I think they perceive me as somebody very fair, from whom you can come and get justice. I think so. I am instinctively a fair-minded person and if I find the justice of a cause demands something, well I do it. If I must say so myself, my relations with the members of the profession are extremely good.

Desiree Bernard is a personable, attractive woman who is very approachable. Her status as judge and eminent lawyer has led to her involvement with women's rights on the international scene. In 1981 she was asked to be the Rapporteur for the United Nations Committee on the elimination of discrimination against women. This committee was established to monitor the progress of women's status in countries throughout the world. In 1985 she was appointed the chair of this important body. The government of Guyana in recognition of this and other achievements gave her one of their highest awards in 1985: the Cacique Crown of Honour.

> I believe that one should always have a goal in life, that you should fix your goal and work towards it, that excellence

should always be the hallmark of achievement in life, whether you are a rice-farmer, a market-vendor or a professional, always aim to be at the top of that field. Never be satisfied with mediocrity.

Her life is a glittering example of women's achievements but it has not been without its costs. Now that she has carved a path, perhaps it will be easier for the next generation of women. Perhaps then, excellence, achievement and outstanding success will be an advantage to a woman rather than a disadvantage.

Elaine Middleton

July 19, 1929
Head, Department of Social Development
Belize Civil Service
Belize

B elize is located in Central America which is the land mass
that connects South America to North America. Belize is
bounded by Mexico and Guatemala and is the only English speaking country in Central America. Previous to 1973, it was known
as British Honduras. It has been a British colony for over one hundred years and attracted the British because of its abundant supplies of logwood and mahogany. Logwood had properties useful

to the English in the making of dyes for their wool. Like most of the British colonies in the Caribbean, Belize has a large population of African descent. They were brought as slaves to Belize to work as loggers. The people of Belize today consist of many ethnic groups. There are Mestizos, Mopan and Kekchi Indians, Mennonites from Germany, Creoles of African descent, Black Caribs, East Indians and Lebanese. The Maya Indians are felt to be the first occupants of Belize as there are still remnants of the great Mayan civilization.

Elaine Middleton was born on July 25, 1929. She was the first woman to head a department in the Civil Service of Belize. Her retirement in 1981 from the service now puts her position as the first female head in the history books; she entered the Civil Service in 1957. It was not then unusual for women to be working in this service. However, almost all the women worked in the administrative stream; they were typists, clerical assistants and stenographers. The highest level a woman could achieve in this stream was assistant secretary. Elaine Middleton did not enter into this stream; she started in the technical stream as a probation officer for young women. It was a position that had to be filled by a woman because men were not allowed to be probation officers for women. Civil servants who were employed in the technical stream could become department heads and beyond that could become permanent secretaries.

When she entered the civil service, Elaine Middleton had already spent ten years as a school teacher. Like many women, it was her childhood ambition to become a teacher, but after ten years she had second thoughts:

> I had taught for a number of years. I taught all the grades, I had spent several years in the upper division, and I just felt that my horizon was getting too narrow. I just wanted to relate to people on a broader scope. I felt that there wasn't much challenge left for me to take up in the teaching profession. It was like doing one thing year in, year out, except that the faces changed, but essentially we were doing the same things.

The move into the Civil Service was a move into social work, and after two years on the job she was sent to Swansea University in Wales for training in social work. She returned and continued to work in the Department of Social Development. In 1962, she was promoted to assistant head of department. Although the post of head of department was vacant twice while she was assistant, she was not appointed as departmental head until 1972. Elaine Middleton was very much aware of her status as the first woman in such a position, but she had become somewhat accustomed to this as she was the first female assistant head of department in the Civil Service. This had given her the experience of often being the only woman in her work environment.

> I found myself very often in a situation where I was the only female, very very often, and I just relate to them as a person. I found that in the beginning they were a little chary of working with you, but once they find out that you can do the job, they get past it.

However, when she was appointed as head she was very conscious of what it meant.

> It made me perform a little bit extra, to make sure that I did the job efficiently, because I was pretty much aware that a lot would depend on what I did in relation to other women being appointed. So I was always conscious of this, that I had to be sure that I did a good job, to make it easier for the other women who would come after me.

After she took over the department, her goal was to improve the level of its operations and to widen its parameters. She consolidated programs underway, and expanded the 4-H Movement in the country with the idea of integrating youth and agriculture. She started a youth development centre for young men who had dropped out of school and needed more training, and expanded the women's programme. Her aim was to set up a women's desk as a mechanism for promoting social and economic activities. She also set up a home for girls with behaviour problems and a home for children in need of care and protection. Her own personal interest had been in the realization of the youth homes for both boys and girls, the children's home and the women's desk. The idea of the women's desk took a great deal of persistence and managing. No one objected to it but there was little real support. With time, she gained this necessary support. When many countries in the region are still working on establishing women's desks — Elaine Middleton took her country a little ahead of the others by establishing one in Belize.

While she established her career as a civil servant of consequence, she married and had three children. She married when she was thirty years old — an age at which many women already had a husband and children. However, marrying at a relatively later age is quite common for women who pursue education and careers.

> It just worked out that way and I felt that if I wanted to have an education I should do that first before I settled down, because if I waited too long I would be so committed to the family, I wouldn't be able to get away.

Managing a career and a marriage is a very serious dual task that often requires painful decisions. One such decision was to go to England and leave her baby behind with her aunt. She herself was raised by her aunt and not by her mother. The opportunity to be trained in social work had come just after she had her first baby. Her choice was either to stay home with the child or continue her career. She knew she had the family support and that the child would be in good hands and well cared for, but it was a very difficult decision to make and one that many women are faced with.

> It never occurred to me to stop working when I got married. Leaving the baby behind was very hard, very, very hard. I had mixed feelings. One minute I said I shouldn't go, the next minute I said I should go, but between our families we managed. When I returned, she was a year and a half.

Women who pursue careers need a great deal of support, particularly if they are married. Elaine Middleton could not have raised three children, have an outstanding career and a harmonious marriage without the support and understanding of her husband.

> My husband is very tolerant, very tolerant, and not too jealous which I am thankful for. As I said I often have to relate to men. I am always in the company of men. I couldn't have achieved what I have without my husband's support. During times of stress I am nearly always called to be working outside, for example during the hurricane when I should be at

home reassuring the children, here am I at the office making sure that people have enough food and clothing provided. I have to be looking after the community rather than my family. Sometimes I work long hours, sometimes I have to stay out and I don't come home and he is very understanding and he takes charge when I am not there, and I feel that if I didn't have that type of person as a husband I would never be able to do what I do.

A husband's support is important to a wife's peace of mind. Additionally, if they have children, their support becomes as important as her husband's. It has been demonstrated in many studies that children are not necessarily adversely affected by their mother's absence from the home, yet many women who work outside the home have a constant concern that they may be neglecting their children. Elaine Middleton has always had her children's understanding:

The children understand. They were born and they found me working, and they found that I had to leave the home and they grew accustomed to it. And this has made them pretty responsible, because they've got to do things for themselves. They have got to make decisions when I am not there and I think it has helped. They may have missed out in some ways because I am not there all the time for them to talk to, but in other ways it has made them a little stronger than if I was there to baby them. Now and again when I have to go to conferences or to be away they will say, 'Again, mommy!'

She carries a low profile; there is nothing ostentatious about her. She does not seek or attract undue attention. She simply gets the job done. There is no question about her leadership. She has her own ideas and is open to listening and to change, but she is not afraid to lead or take the initiative. She felt that she had to work; it was never a question in her mind. Outside of short training trips abroad, she stayed in Belize and made her contribution by increasing community services to her people and by plugging away tirelessly in the Civil Service. One example of her unwavering dedication is the establishment of the women's desk.

I just wanted to see women treated more or less as equals rather than subordinates. I want to see them have the opportunity to get the kind of education, to do the kind of things that they have the capabilities to do and to really improve their own self-image, because I think many women here think too little of themselves. Their self-esteem is very low. Previously I had placed a lot of emphasis on youth. Since last year I have shifted my emphasis quite a good bit to women and their concerns and I think once I can get one or two good programmes going in that direction, then I think I could shift to adult education generally with special emphasis on the males, because we have got to train and educate the males just as much as the females.

Apart from her own desire to work and contribute, Elaine Middleton was able to pursue her professional interests because her family was supportive. Yet it was for them that she worked.

I want my children to have a good life. I want them to have a good education, because I feel that we don't have any money. We don't have any property to pass on to them, but we can give them a good basic education, they can take it from there. And I think this is one of the reasons why I keep on working — because I want to give my children a better chance in life than I started out with.

These sentiments are felt by most parents. A good education is part of many Caribbean parents' dream for their children. Everyone struggles for it. Elaine Middleton has given her children education and she has given her country conscientious and diligent service. She may not have money or property to leave her children, but she has something more important to leave them — her name and her contribution; both are marked by integrity and respect, wrought from a life of service to her country.

Louise Rowley

March 25, 1912
Permanent Secretary
Grenada

During the 1924 Junior Cambridge Examination in Grenada, the Examiner was taken aback by the presence of a little girl. He noted her for two reasons; one was that she was too little to reach the desk so that she could comfortably write her exam papers; and books had to be found for her to sit on. The second was that she had two braids with bows; all the girls had their hair "up".

> At that time in Grenada, as soon as you were fifteen, you
> combed you hair up and you put on long stockings because,
> you see, before that you were wearing socks.

The girls who sat for these exams were usually fifteen years old.
However, this particular girl was only twelve years old; her name
was Louise Rowley. She was born in Toko Bay, a small village in
St. David's, Grenada, on the 25th of March, 1912. Her father was
a schoolteacher who left for Brazil in search of better opportunities. He died there before Louise was born, and she and her
elder sister and brother were raised by their mother who became
a Nurse/Midwife after her husband died. She was posted as the
first District Nurse in Guauve, where she raised her three
children.

Ms. Rowley and her sister went to the St. John's Anglican School
and her mother, who was strict, raised them to feel that they were
special. As a Nurse, her salary was 19s.11d (US$4.78).

> We never felt deprived; we were poor, but we were happy.
> Mum was a wonderful lady.

Her mother stressed education and discipline. By the time
Louise Rowley was eighteen years old, she was the most highly
qualified woman in Grenada. She was later to be among the first
permanent secretaries in the region and the first female permanent secretary in the Caribbean. Louise passed the Junior Cambridge Examination when she was twelve years old, passed the
School-Leaving Certificate Examination at fifteen and placed third
in the London Matriculation Examination at seventeen. The
School Certificate Examination is equivalent to the "O" Level Examinations, and the London Matriculation was the Examination
taken to win the Leeward Islands Scholarship which was offered
every two years.

This Scholarship was previously offered to the boy who placed
highest in the Examination. Ms. Rowley was the first woman in
Grenada to pass these Examinations. The objective of a girl's
education was to make her a good wife and mother. Schools for
girls were finishing schools. Rather than algebra, girls were taught
how to sew; rather than geometry, girls were taught how to em-
broider; rather than history, girls were taught home economics
and good manners. It was because a girl's education was struc-

tured so differently from a boy's that Scholarships were offered only to boys.

When Louise Rowley passed the London Matriculation, they wrote about her in the newspapers.

> It was quite a talk in town; it was a sensation, and everybody would hail me, but nobody said, '... and here is a job.'

In fact, when she passed the London Matriculation, she went to all the business enterprises looking for a job.

> I had the highest qualifications that were available in Grenada. I was the first woman to have these qualifications. I came into town; I walked with all my qualifications, you know, trying to impress. I first went to the private sector and they all looked at them and they were impressed with the Certificates. They said I had all of these Certificates but I didn't have the right ones — I didn't have shorthand and typing. So I decided to apply to the Government.

Her mother had applied for her earlier when she had her Junior Cambridge and School-Leaving Certificates.

> The entrance requirement for the Civil Service at the time was Cambridge Junior. I had Cambridge Senior (School-Leaving Certificate). When I had Matriculation and I applied again, they gave me a job as sorter in the Post Office. So I took that job; that was what was available.

At the time Louise Rowley applied to the Civil Service, there were only three classifications for women in the Civil Service — copier, typist and a sorter in the Post Office. Everyone sorted the mail; even the Postmaster himself. Sorting was just a job category under which women could be employed. Because these categories were of a lower rank in the Civil Service, they were, of course, at a lower salary — even though as a sorter a woman could be doing the work of a clerk.

The Civil Service then was a male-dominated institution. Employment as a clerk was possible for a man at five different levels; a junior clerk would start at a Clerk 5 position and a senior clerk would be a Clerk 1. Because a woman could not move up beyond sorter, it was not possible for her to advance to the top job in the Civil Service which was that of Permanent Secretary.

As a sorter, Ms. Rowley became the Postmaster's correspondence clerk.

> At that time, you know, I was so simple and innocent, it never occurred to me I was being kept down, that I was being discriminated against. Here I was, having higher qualifications than any man in the Civil Service, and here I was in the post of a sorter in the Post Office. If a man had the same qualifications, he would have entered at least at the Clerk 3 level. It never occurred to me to revolt or to write or complain. I was happy just to do my work and I never felt I was being oppressed. I am amazed at myself now.

She worked at this post for several years until one year the Postmaster was on leave and the Colonial Treasurer acted as Postmaster.

> In those days, most of our mail used to go through Trinidad and we used to pay Trinidad every July based on the statistics of every piece of mail. One year, we didn't know what happened to the statistics, but the bill that was presented was completely out of proportion to what was normally received. Now Mr. Beaubrun, the Treasurer, was the acting Postmaster; he was a man who had no uses for women, no way. He didn't want a woman in his office. So when this bill came down from Trinidad, he didn't want to pay it. He asked me to look into it, you know treasurers don't like to pay money. French was my favourite subject in school, so to keep it up I used to read all the French notes and regulations which came from the Universal Postal Union, and I remember reading in one of them that if there was something out of the normal in the statistics, then the country you are paying should reduce the charge. When I told Mr. Beaubrun this, he was so happy that he had me send a letter to Trinidad right away. They said no. We wrote them again. They said no again to reducing the charge. I suggested to him that a letter should be sent to the Secretary of State in London, who did agree with us and reduced the charge by 600 Pounds. Well, that is nothing now but then 600 Pounds was a lot of money.

Mr. Beaubrun was so impressed by Ms. Rowley that he promoted her to a Class 5 Clerk. This was unprecedented. The rules were not changed because Ms. Rowley was promoted; an exception was made. Since he was the Colonial Treasurer, he wanted her in the Treasury and, as soon as there was a vacancy in the Treasury, he appointed her.

So I left the women and went to the Treasury. The Treasury was a bastion of male supremists. I was the only female there. I remember the first day I walked in, this man said 'change and decay all around I see.'[1] I can't say they didn't receive me and they said that at last they're glad to see a woman come in, but they weren't taking me seriously. They were selecting what they were giving me to do. If the person before me was doing that, they took it away. I said no way, I said nothing doing. Everything that my predecessor was doing I want to do, no matter what it is. You see these men; I'm going to show them that a woman is going to do this job just as them, even, I said to myself, better than them.

Slowly Ms. Rowley established herself as a worker of quality in the Civil Service. It was difficult; they would keep information from her and she would go out of her way to learn everything there was to know, studying all the regulations, reading everything. Finally they accepted that she was capable.

After a time when the men realized that I was capable, they started to call me Mr. Rowley as if to say she is a woman but she's not really a woman; and that used to annoy me. Doing things good, you ceased to be a woman.

She has always been conscious of her responsibility to other women, particularly in her effort to be an example of women's ability and place in the Civil Service of Grenada.

Well, they abolished the three categories of sorter, copier and typist for women workers and introduced 'a lady clerk'. I used to speak about it at every meeting of the Civil Service Association. It is time to get rid of this kind of discrimination — we should accept women in the Civil Service on the same basis as men. Why must men be accepted as clerks and women be accepted 'lady clerks'?

The "lady clerk" category was abolished before 1956 and this heralded a new day when women could enter the Civil Service on the basis of their qualifications.

Louise Rowley's life in the Civil Service spanned almost forty years from 1930 to 1969.

She gained a reputation as an excellent worker and advanced to the Clerk 1 position and beyond. By the time self-government began in 1956 in Grenada, when Grenadians took over responsibility from England for administering the island's affairs, she was in the position to become one of three persons selected to become Permanent Secretaries.

The Civil Service in the Caribbean is the body which operates the Institutions of the Governments. The Ministry of Education, for example, must ensure that teachers are employed, enough schools are available, standards of education are kept and that curricula are relevant to the needs of the country. The person in charge of this is the Minister, and overseeing this process for the Minister as well as advising the Minister is the Permanent Secretary — the highest post in the Civil Service.

This was the first time that the Ministerial system was going to be used in Grenada. There were to be three Ministries; the Ministry of Works and Communication, the Ministry of Social Services and the Ministry of Agriculture. The three persons appointed as Permanent Secretaries were; Louise Rowley, George Holston and Gordon St. Bernard. Becoming a Permanent Secretary in 1956 made Louise Rowley the first woman to become a Permanent Secretary in the Caribbean. She was a pioneer for women in the Civil Service. It was not until the late '60s that women began to emerge in this position in the Region. It was only recently that female Permanent Secretaries in the Caribbean have increased to a noticeable number.

Louise Rowley chose not to marry. Outside of the Civil Service, she was devoted to social work in the Church and in the Red Cross where she has served with distinction as Secretary since 1955, and to raising two adopted children. Her life has been filled with love. She was seventy-five years old on 25th March 1987, but she looks at least twenty years younger. She and her seventy-seven year old sister, Doris, also as youthful, live in Grand Anse. In the evenings, Doris sits and tats — a kind of lace-making very rarely done or taught today, and Louise embroiders. She is excellent in embroidery and will soon have an exhibition of her work, and may even teach an embroidery class. This woman, who sits on her verandah and embroiders, was a feminist, a pioneer for women in the Civil Service.

I feel that what I did as a woman hastened the day when women became accepted on legal terms as men in the Civil

Service. That is why Grenada has led the field in the acceptance of women in the Civil Service. Now there are four female Permanent Secretaries.

In 1966, she received the O.B.E. Award. The citation read as follows:

> Louise Rowley, who joined the Grenada Civil Service in 1930 as a very junior clerk, has served in numerous departments of Government and has, by dint of hard and conscientious work, now deservedly risen to the top rank of the Service.
> Notwithstanding the arduous and exacting duties of her post, she always found time to go over and above her duties in the field of social work. Miss Rowley is a woman of exceptional ability and character, and serves as an outstanding example to the women of Grenada and one of whom they may be justly proud.

Louise Rowley retired in 1969. Her forty years in the Civil Service is her legacy to all Grenadians but particularly to the women, not only of Grenada, but the whole Caribbean. She is, above all, a devoted daughter of Grenada. "I love to travel, but I love to come back. There is nowhere else except Grenada."

¹This quote is from the Hymn *Abide with Me*.

Bernice Edna Yorke

July 6, 1921
Teacher
Belize

The positions of teaching, nursing and secretary have traditionally been among the very few careers open to women. As a result, women who sought careers automatically went into these fields.

These positions are not highly paid nor do they wield great power. Yet they provide needed and essential services. In the Caribbean, an education provides a child with the means to respectability. It was easy to become a teacher if you passed

enough subjects. Although being a teacher did not entitle you
to a large fortune, it did entitle you to respect from your community and peers, and it never failed to make parents proud to
know that their son or daughter had become a teacher.

Bernice Edna Yorke became a teacher. She was born in Belize
City, Belize. Today she runs her own infant school with a reputation for its excellence in drama. Every year Bernie Yorke enters
her students in the National Belize Festival of Arts and every year
of the past eight her students have won every prize in all of the
categories in which they competed. She has had no formal training in art or drama. She became involved in drama as the eldest
child in a family of eight children. Her father would read
Shakespeare to them and they would put on little plays at home.
She also spent a lot of time with an aunt who produced plays.
She was fascinated by acting and drama and the person who encouraged her interest was her father.

> I became interested in drama very, very early in life. I always
> liked to perform, although I was very nervous. I always liked
> to act, liked to recite. Every time I would recite I would never
> look at the audience. I was always shaking, but I did it. And I
> was always producing for my sisters, my brothers and my
> friends. My father was the president of the literary and
> dramatic club and he produced plays and he was always
> reading Shakespeare for us.

She was nineteen years old when her family was shattered by
the death of her father. As there were eight children who were
still quite young and in school, the older children in the family
began to take on the financial responsibility for the household.
As the eldest child, Bernice Yorke began teaching immediately
after her father's death. She taught in one-room schools. There
were about forty to fifty students in the one-room school and
the teacher taught all subjects to all students. She moved to different schools in her teaching career and it was when she moved
to another school as assistant principal that she met her husband,
then principal. They married and had two children, a son and
a daughter.

Bernice Yorke's school was not started until 1966. After many
years of teaching in the public school system, she decided to

teach privately. One evening she was at a party where some of the women were complaining.

> The ladies expressed their grave concern about wanting to send their little children to school and they had nowhere to send them. And they turned to me and they said, 'Mrs. Yorke, why don't you start a kindergarten school?' Of course I laughed and I said, well it's a good idea and I'll think about it, and I decided that it was a good idea.

A few months later the downstairs of a building in her neighbourhood became vacant and she decided to lease it and start the school. She invested her savings in equipment, desks and chairs, and opened the school in September 1966. She had sent letters out to parents informing them of the school's opening. When she opened she had twenty-four children registered. The charge per child was five dollars per month. Today she has over a hundred children in her school. Her school is one of the few private kindergartens in Belize and also one of the established ones. Her focus on art came about not only because she was interested in it, but because she felt that it was a way to teach the children about life.

> I think it's very important for the children to get exposed to the arts very early and it does help them. It widens their horizons and it gives them a chance to project themselves. Out of this I hope we will get our future leaders of the country.

The children study dance, recitation, acting, drama and learn of the importance of being responsible for their roles and of projecting one's self. Bernice Yorke teaches well and with care. It is not easy to get a five year old child to remember lines, but if she is playing a duchess then she will remember those lines because she is suddenly adult and important. The children love her and they love the acting and the drama. But the constant outstanding performance is not without its price.

One year Bernice Yorke produced a play and entered the adult drama competition. She won. Not only had she won all the prizes she competed for in the children's section of the festival, she had won the drama prize in the adult section.

Many people have said, well as long as Mrs. Yorke is doing this we haven't got a chance. I think that I have been instrumental in helping those who have done this to work a little harder and strive for higher standards. Some people tell them, well Mrs. Yorke works hard. I wish I could give up and leave the field open to them, but I cannot do that and remain in Belize. I am not going to jeopardize my children, and I am not going to refrain from exposing them or helping them to do these things because of others. I am sorry.

There are many facets to this woman. For example, she is a Bahai. Although the Bahai faith is not as well known as Christianity or Islam, it too had its origins in the Middle East, and it has followers in almost every part of the world. There is a strong Bahai group in Belize and Bernice Yorke has been the chair and vice-chair of the National Spiritual Assembly for several years. The Spiritual Assembly is the main organizational body of the faith. Unlike many religions, it can be headed by a woman. Bahai believe in the oneness of God, Man and Religion. One of the most striking differences between the Bahai religion and other religions is the tenet that there must be equal status for both men and women. Abdu'l-Baha, one of the central figures of the faith, wrote:

> The world of humanity has two wings as it were, one is the female, the other is the male. If one wing is defective the strong perfect wing will not be capable of flight. The world of humanity has two hands. If one be imperfect, the capable hand is restricted and unable to perform its duties. God is the creator of mankind. He has endowed both sexes with perfections and intelligence, given them physical members and organs of sense, without differentiation or distinction as to superiority, therefore why should women be considered inferior? This is not according to the plan and justice of God. He has created them equal; in His estimate there is no question of sex.

Bernice Yorke became a Bahai when she was forty years old. She had become disillusioned with the Christian faith and was looking for alternative philosophies.

> I realized that it had the answers for my questions. I was very deeply involved in the church and I was disillusioned. I tried to live the Christian faith and I didn't get this response from

people who should have been setting the example. It was my father who pointed out to me that Christianity was not the only religion, many many years ago when I was growing up. When we were taught at church that everything else was heathen except Christianity. That didn't make sense to me, but I had no answers and I had to accept it for then. And he told me of the Muslim faith. He had apparently studied comparative religion. He told me that they were very devout people, they know they must pray five fimes a day. They do it. Are you going to tell me that God isn't for those people too, only just Christians? So this sort of opened my eyes.

Bernice Yorke is a fascinating woman. She is a tall woman with a brilliant smile and a wonderful presence. Her talents as an artist and teacher have always been recognized and applauded. She does not have enough room for all the prizes and awards she has received. On getting to know her one would think that she should be an actress in New York rather than a school teacher in Belize. She certainly has the same talent, passion and individuality. She is not afraid to be different, whether it is being almost scandalously successful, or the follower of a religion not understood or known by most people in the region.

I always say that one should be oneself. I say it a lot but I don't really understand it. I mean if I am a worthless good-for-nothing person, that is what I must be? I think it needs to be qualified. Find out what the best in you is, and do that. Now I don't know how you find this out. I think you have to measure yourself against very high standards and see how you do. My philosophy is that I should try to do the best I can as long as I can.

The state of the arts in Belize is in an embryonic stage. There are those in Belize who are struggling to keep it alive. Bernice Yorke is one of those. Sometimes it is a struggle, and sometimes the rewards make it worthwhile, but most of the time it is a hard, lonely task. For Bernice Yorke, the innocence, the eagerness and enthusiasm of the children provide her sustenance and hope.

It is the children, without them I couldn't make it.

Isabel Belgrove Sealy

May 26, 1882
Domestic
Barbados

I sabel Belgrove Sealy was walking slowly up the road in the parish of St. John, Barbados.

> I walk and go up. If a bus come before nine I got to pay. I walk, you mean just from here up de road, pass de burial ground and go up and I have to pay a bus — not even an hour.

Walking in the hot sun for an hour is not an unaccustomed hardship for Isabel Sealy. When she was a young woman in her twenties, she made her living by selling and logged many miles.

> I would walk with a tray on my head and the people when
> they see me they would stop me and I would sell them.

Her "not even an hour" walk is something she does almost every day and it takes her an hour because she has been slowed by her one hundred years.

She was born on a Wednesday, on the 26th day of May 1882 in the parish of St. John, Barbados. Her father was a coachman and her mother a cook in the estate home. She went as far as the fourth year in primary school and left school to work. Mother of six children, Isabel Sealy is a vibrant and active woman. She remembers Barbados as it used to be and regrets that people no longer like to plant in Barbados.

> I used to plant potato and cassava, you can't get nice potatoes
> now; you see people don't want to plant. It was good when I
> was young, because everything was plentiful and nice and
> everybody going along pretty and nice pon de street.

Although she had her own plot of land and planted and sold her produce, this was only one of the jobs that she held to raise her children. After the emancipation of the slaves, many women left the plantations and took up huckstering as a way of making a living. In her book *Women of Barbados* Jill Hamilton refers to the work of historian Richard Ligon:

> *He writes of women hucksters; who sold sundry items ranging
> from produce they grew such as ground provisions to crabs
> they caught, along with homemade goods as well as imported
> items consisting of coals, bundles of shingles, haberdashery
> and other fancy goods. Some of them traded from door to
> door with baskets or trays balanced on their heads, others
> with push carts (as is the custom throughout Barbados to this
> day) and the remainder had shops which varied in size. (p.15)*

Isabel Sealy worked alone. With her mother and father's help she raised her six children. She never married. With each of the two men in her life she had three children. When those relationships ended. She became the sole support for the children.

> I put a tray on my head and I sell potato, I sell cassava and I
> sell yam. I did some of everything to keep my children decent
> on the road.

After a while, she gave up huckstering and became a domestic. Domestic work was once done by slaves. It was a desirable task because it was not as physically strenuous as field work. The black woman as a domestic worker first appeared in Barbados in the 1640s.

> It is at this point in the Island's history that African women were brought in great numbers to work in the sugar cane fields and a few taken into the homes of the more wealthy planters and merchants as domestic workers. (Hamilton, p.18)

This domestic work evolved into paid work after emancipation. These jobs were, however, very poorly paid. Isabel Sealy's first domestic job paid her four dollars per week. When she retired her pay was seventeen dollars per week.

Isabel Sealy worked for one family for over forty-five years. Her job was to "cook, wash, iron and mind nine children." Her primary job was taking care of the children. Many women who worked as domestics were nannies. Although the family treated her with respect and affection, it was difficult because she "lived in," taking care of nine children while her own were at home being raised by her mother.

> Sometimes you workin and you frettin all de time, you frettin all de time. But I tend to my children, I tend to my children, tend to my children good too.

These competing demands of work and children are a part of the lives of all working women who have children. Isabel Sealy had to adjust to the fact that she had to live in another person's home taking care of their children while her own children were at home without her. The economic realities of her life did not allow her to do as she wished. In order to earn enough to take care of her children this was what she had to do. One of the things that made it easier for her was that her children were older by the time she started her job as a live-in nanny. It was not long before they reached adulthood, and this lifted from her some of the weight of worrying.

The work of a domestic is difficult both physically and emotionally. It requires an ability to take orders and to do some frequently unpleasant tasks. Sometimes the person in charge of the domestic or nanny is insensitive and disrespectful, not recognizing her value. The work of a domestic, whether she be nanny, cook or maid, is as important as any other work.

Domestic work is very needed. Such workers are not only important to those who need this service but important to the society and to the economy of the country. They contribute their skills and labour like any other worker in the society.

> House servants were an integral part of the island's whole social and economic structure ... nannies were especially devoted to their 'charges' and often exerted as much or more influence on the child than its parents. We are greatly indebted to all those who served and serve in that capacity.
> (Hamilton, p. 48)

The children that Isabel Sealy raised have grown up to take on various jobs in Barbados and abroad. They regard her with affection, for it was she who woke up at night to tend to their needs and it was she who saw them through infancy, childhood, adolescence to adulthood.

> Them is the children that I raise. Them is like mine. They come and look for me. They don't leave me out, they don't leave me out in nothing at all. When they come to visit me everything that they can find to bring they bring. They good to me up to now.

In the morning she would fix their porridge, get them dressed and take them for a walk. As they grew older, she made their breakfast and got them ready for school. While they were at school, she would do chores around the house: dusting, sweeping and ironing. She took charge after they returned home, and made sure that they ate their meals and did their homework. She was there for them to complain to, talk to, and to settle disputes for them.

Her life, although marked by hard work and sacrifice, had its moments of lightness and happiness. Her favorite pastime was dancing. In the early nineteen hundreds when she was a young woman, the dances were quite different; reggae and soca were not even thought of. In her day, Isabel Sealy could be seen on the floor trying all the latest dance steps:

Flame figures, Caledonian, two step, lancers, quadrille and the change-off flirt. I like the quadrille and the change-off flirt best. You dash youself this way and you turn this way and you change off, and you go round and you swing and you go round. I had a good time dancing.

She says to "wine up is dancin to kill youself." Even though she is over a hundred years old she still gets on the floor when the occasion demands.

They had a thing there for me the other night and I get up then and put it pon de floor.

She recalls the days when she was the dancer to watch.

Dance? Dance? If I could dance? I ain't see nobody who could do more dancin than me. When you see me pon de floor you will have to sit down and watch.

She lives with her daughter in St. John's parish in Barbados where she has lived all her life. She is a devout churchgoer at St. John's Anglican church. She has an animated and beautifully wrinkled face. Her body is thin and wiry and it almost jumps on its own to show the change-off flirt when she talks about dancing. When she goes on her daily walk, those who know her often stop their cars and give her a lift. Everyone greets her on the street. "Mornin, Miss Sealy" or "Good afternoon, Miss Sealy" or "Hello, Miss Sealy." At her hundredth birthday Isabel Sealy was on television. The newspapers wrote about her and many Barbadians heard about and saw her for the first time. She can still dance, can walk to her destination with ease and remembers the events of her life as clearly as if they happened yesterday. In the parish of St. John, she is a well respected woman. "I don't think somebody would have something bad to say about Miss Sealy."

Isabel Sealy says that she was able to reach the age of 100 because "I ain't give no rush. I does take everything cool. Everything I take cool, cool, cool."

She has seen Barbados move from coach to bus and from quadrille to reggae. In many ways she is Barbados — one of those people who built Barbados. What is impressive is that she did so in work that has gone unrecognized. Who will know when Isabel Sealy dies that she danced the quadrille, that she regrets that "Barbadians don't plant no particular potatoes anymore" and that she put a tray on her head to keep her children "decent on the road."

There have been many women like Isabel Sealy. Not many have lived as long as she, but they served their country and their families and passed on forgotten because they were not "the leaders of the country". It is women like Isabel Sealy, struggling to survive and to raise and educate their children, who built the foundations of their countries.

I didn't have nothing. I get by, somehow I get by.

As a nanny she raised nine children. She is the mother of six children, and has fourteen grand-, twenty-four great-grand- and five great-great-grandchildren. This woman, Isabel Belgrove Sealy, is a builder of Barbados.

Glossary

Ackee:* The scarlet pear-shaped fruit of the tree *Blighia sapida*. It splits open when ripe and its cream-coloured flesh is edible. The National Fruit of Jamaica.

Atilla: 19th Century Calypsonian in Trinidad.

Bahai Faith: A belief that recognizes the unity of God and his prophets. Teaches that divine revelation is continuous and progressive, and that the founders of all past religions though different in the non-essential aspects of their teachings proclaim the same spiritual truth.

Barrister: A member of the legal profession who pleads cases in court.

Beirut: Capital of Lebanon.

Belair* (Dominica, Grenada, St. Lucia): A carnival folk dance led by a solo singer (the Chanterelle) who dances backwards giving the time to the drummer.

Black Caribs: Still exist in Dominica, St. Vincent and Belize; are the descendants of Caribs who intermarried with escaped slaves.

British Council Scholarship: The British Council was formed in the 1930s. One of its main functions was to give scholarships to non-British persons.

Bustamante, Sir Alexander: First Prime Minister of Jamaica, from 1962-1967.

Caledonian:* A popular Scottish dance adopted by Creole Societies in the West Indies of the late 1800s and early 1900s.

Caribs: The Caribs and Arawaks were the original inhabitants of the Caribbean.

Cassava: The root of a shrubby plant grown in the tropics and eaten for its fleshy rootstock which yields a nutritious starch.

Castries: Capital of St. Lucia.

Change-off Flirt:* A movement in which the dancers made a display of grace in changing the steps between varieties of Lancers.

Channa: Also called chick peas or garbanzo beans. Channa is an east Indian word and is made in various ways in the Caribbean. It can be boiled or fried with garnish or it can be curried or salted and served like peanuts.

Chanterelle:* The woman singer and dancer who leads the belair, giving the lead line to a chorus in which she introduces sharp social satire.

Chinese in the Caribbean: Colonial Office record 295/2/ records that 100 Chinese were landed in Trinidad in 1802. It was an experiment to develop Trinidad without slaves. Very strong anti-slavery sentiments were building in England at that time.

Coast Guard: A military or naval force employed in guarding a coast.

Cold Supper Shop* (Jamaican): A shop selling cooked food such as fritters, roast breadfruit, corn pone and other items normally bought by workers for their midday snack.

Cornwall: Located in the Southwest tip of England.

Creoles: In Belize, the descendants of Africans.

Cutlass:* A sharp iron blade about two feet in length with slight upward curve at the tip and fitted with a wooden handle, for cutting canes, chopping limbs, etc.

Daal Puri:* A type of roti with a light filling of "Daal", a paste made of split peas boiled, ground and slightly seasoned.

Dame: A female member of an order of Knighthood.

Dinkyminnie* (Jamaica): "A type of ring-play or dancing usually practised in connection with funeral ceremonies; also the ceremonies themselves." (Dictionary of Jamaican English, CUP, 1980)

Driver* (Sugar Industry): 1. *(In history)* A trusted slave in charge of a labour gang of slaves whom he controlled with a whip. 2. *(Later)* An assistant to the overseer who gives orders to a small work-force on a sugar estate.

Dasheen*: A large edible tuber of the eddoe family, slightly slimy when boiled.

Eric Williams: 1911-1981. Prime Minister of Trinidad.

Extemporaneous verses: Verses made up on the spur of the moment.

External Student:* One who studies for an English University degree or professional certificate by correspondence, and usually without going to England.

Feminism: The theory of the political, economic and social equality of women. Organized activities on behalf of women's rights and interests.

Foreman* (Sugar Industry): The man immediately in charge of the mechanics or machine-workmen in a sugar factory.

Gender Specific: Gender specific refers to activities which only one sex, one gender performs.

Hayricks: A large heap of hay.

Hurricane David: One of the worst hurricanes in the Caribbean. It struck Dominica on August 30, 1979, killing twenty-two people and leaving 60,000 homeless.

Improvisatori: One who can perform on the spur of the moment a musical or dramatic composition.

Indentured Labour:* The system by which immigrant labourers were imported from the Indian sub-continent, under agreement or "indenture", to replace slave-labour in the West Indies after Emancipation.

Kaiso:* The original folk name for what later came to be called calypso.

Kekchi or **Quekchi:** An Indian people of the Mayan civilization.

Last Rites: Final rites and prayers for a dying person.

Lancers: A set of five quadrilles each in a different meter.

Licks: A flogging; a beating; blows.

Lime* (Eastern Caribbean): To stand around in groups on the sidewalk or any likely meeting place, chatting and commenting on passers-by; to meet at a friend's house to sit and pass the time away; to stand around idly.

Madam Iree: The only female calypsonian in Trinidad in the 1940s and 1950s.

Manley, Norman: Chief Minister of Jamaica 1955-1959; Premier of Jamaica 1959-1962.

Manley, Michael: Prime Minister of Jamaica 1972-1981.

Maternity Benefits: Benefits due to a woman who has to be away from the workplace because of pregnancy and childbirth.

Moors: Open rolling wasteland, marshy and covered with heather.

Mud house:* A small dwelling made of a strengthened framework of dried limbs and ends of wood plastered over with smooth mud and covered with a thatched roof.

One-room school: The one-room or one-teacher school is a feature of the early periods in a country's development. It is present today in many rural areas of the world and in many developing countries.

Nominated member: A person who is nominated to hold a seat in Parliament, rather than elected.

Nurse-Midwife: A nurse whose main job is assisting women in childbirth.

Ordained minister: A minister invested with the functions of that office.

Overseer* (Sugar Industry): Usually young white man in charge of the work-force in a large section of a sugar plantation which he supervises often on mule-back.

Phagwah*: A religious Hindu holiday.

Ph.D.: Abbreviation for a doctorate in philosophy — an advanced degree attained at a University. It requires previous University degrees usually at the Bachelor of Arts or Masters level.

Piti Belle Lily, Alice Sugar, Mossie Millie, Ocean Lizzie, Sybil Steele, Darling Dan and **Ling Mama:** Names of women who performed calypso in the 19th century.

Pocomania* (Jamaica): A religious practice of black Jamaicans involving ancestor-worship, spirit-possession, singing and speaking in tongues.

Puja: A word used for ritual prayer in Hinduism.

Quadrille: A square dance for four couples made up of five or six figures.

Quality control: A system devised to ensure that products made in a factory are of a certain acceptable standard of quality.

Quekchi: see kekchi.

Racism: The belief in the inherent superiority of one race over all others and thereby the right to dominance.

Reggae:* "A type of music developed in Jamaica about 1964, usually having a heavy four-beat rhythm, using the bass, electric guitar, and drum, with the scraper coming in at the end of the measure and acting as accompaniment to emotional songs often expressing rejection of established 'white-man' culture." (Dictionary of Jamaican English, CUP, 1980).

Robeson, Paul: Great Black American actor, singer, athlete and scholar. Noted for his outspoken stand on racial discrimination in the United States of America.

Royal Academy of Dramatic Arts: The most prestigious academy of arts in Great Britain.

Sangster, Sir Donald: Acting Prime Minister of Jamaica (1966-1967).

Scotch: A person born in Scotland.

Senior Cambridge: Examinations set for senior high school students in the British Colonies — set by the Oxford and Cambridge system in England.

Sexism: The belief in the inherent superiority of one sex and thereby the right to dominance.

Shilling: A British monetary unit.

Soca* (Trinidad): A song and dance tune combining the rhythm and beat of Black American "soul" and Trinidadian "calypso", emerging in the late 1970s with "Sugar Bum" as a popular example.

Solicitor: A member of the legal profession who is not a barrister. Involved mainly in legal research.

Sparrow: Sometimes described as the greatest calypsonian.

Susu* (Trinidad): A cooperative saving scheme called "partners" in Jamaica. See "Throwing Partners".

Swansea University: University located in Wales.

Tanty*: An affectionate term for aunt.

Teaching restrictions: In many Caribbean territories, women who were married had to give up their teaching posts.

Throwing Box* (Guyana) or **Throwing Partners*** (Jamaica): Joining in a friendly cooperative saving scheme limited to a small number of persons, of whom each contributes the same agreed weekly sum to the organizer who passes the amount accumulated each week to a different member of the group in turn.

Toast Mistress Club: An organization whose objectives are the development of leadership and public speaking skills for women.

Tram Car: A street car which ran on rails laid in the public road. Once the major means of transportation in Jamaica and Guyana.

Two Step: A ballroom dance executed with a sliding step — close-step in march or polka time.

Wholesale: The selling of goods in large quantities, usually at lower prices.

Wine Up* (Wind Up): (Especially of women) to dance (to music with a quick beat) by twisting the body in vigorous snake-like movements from side to side and back and forth, especially below the waist.

Women's desk: A governmental position responsible for overseeing the affairs of women.

Women's Education: Schools in the Caribbean were established primarily for boys. It was felt that sewing and other domestic subjects were important for the girls' education. This was often the only means used to encourage girls' education.

Y.W.C.A. in Africa: The oldest Y.W.C.A. organizations in Africa are between 25 to 35 years old.

*The glossing of these items has been supplied by Dr. Richard Allsopp, coordinator, Caribbean Lexicography Project, UWI at Cave Hill, Barbados. The material forms part of the draft of a *Dictionary of Caribbean English Usage* in preparation.

About the Author

NESHA HANIFF was born and raised in Guyana. She received her Ph.D. in Education from the University of Michigan where she is currently Visiting Assistant Professor at the Centre for Afro-American and Caribbean Studies. Her research continues to focus on Caribbean women.